DREAMHEALER

Known only as ADAM, the author is
a young and incredibly gifted dis-
tant-energy healer.

Also by Adam

DreamHealer 2: A Guide to Healing and Self-Empowerment

The Path of the DreamHealer

DreamHealer

A True Story
of Miracle Healings

ADAM

TIME WARNER
BOOKS

This edition published in Great Britain in 2006 by Time Warner Books
First published by DreamHealer Inc. in 2003
Published by Penguin Group (Canada), a division of Pearson
Penguin Canada Inc., in 2006

A CIP catalogue record for this book is available from the British Library.

ISBN-13: 978-0-7515-3842-7
ISBN-10: 0-7515-3842-6

Typeset in Minion by M Rules
Printed and bound in Great Britain by
Clays Ltd, St Ives plc

Time Warner Books
An imprint of
Little, Brown Book Group
Brettenham House
Lancaster Place
London WC2E 7EN

A member of the Hachette Livre Group of Companies

www.littlebrown.co.uk

Time Warner Books is a trademark of Time Warner Inc. or
an affiliated company. Used under licence by Little, Brown Book Group,
which is not affiliated with Time Warner Inc.

Contents

Acknowledgments

I would like to express my gratitude to everyone who contributed to the making of this book by having the courage and open-mindedness to try something different. It has been an inspirational process every step of the way. Thanks to Dr. Effie Chow and Dr. Edgar Mitchell for their encouraging words of wisdom. Thanks to my sister for being herself and, most of all, thanks to my mom and dad for believing in me.

The Dream

THE DREAM is a mystical connection with universal energy, which expands life's perspective to a non-ordinary state of consciousness.

We interpret our reality through our five senses: sight, sound, smell, taste and touch. Our awareness is therefore based on very little input if we evaluate it only through those five sensory input areas. With our eyes, we see only a very small part of the electromagnetic spectrum. We hear only a fraction of the known frequency range. And we have no way of quantifying the amount or range perceived from our sense of smell, taste and touch senses.

But we are still bombarded with input, whether it is measurable or not. It is fair to assume that we have some awareness of it, and react to it. Therefore it is subjective sensitivity that interprets all of our sensory data. This leaves the door open for the extended human capacity to process information such as intuition, feelings, visions and dreams.

The dream is our vision of perfect health.

The healer is our guide along this path.

—Adam

Chapter I
Discovery

To perceive beyond ourselves is to truly see.

—ADAM·

God must have a sense of humor. I don't know how else to explain the irony of my placement on this planet.

I was born into a regular middle-class family in a large cosmopolitan city. About 30 percent of the area's population is of Chinese descent, and had I been born into a home within this community, the cultural channels of Qigong or Taoism would embrace my uniqueness. It would be accepted as a rarity, not an oddity. The main thing is that it would be accepted.

The next largest visible minority in my city is East Indian, and if I had been born into this culture,

I might have been spirited away to an ashram for mentoring. Again, the culture recognizes uncommon talents such as mine as gifts to be honed and developed. They are not only accepted; they are respected.

In contrast, the beliefs and customs of the Western culture to which I was assigned do not seem to welcome that which is not common. It purports to celebrate individualism, though in reality what is accepted is sameness. It is a culture that likes everyone to do the same thing, to be similar. Different is viewed as strange. At best, it is tolerated. What is valued is what we can process with the five senses and not anything beyond them. In Western culture, reality must be measurable.

I was born with a red birthmark shaped like a V on the center of my forehead. I have been told this is the "mark of a healer" because it is located on what is called the third eye. The third eye is where a healer channels his energy to connect with others for healing purposes. The V mark has faded considerably: It can barely be seen now, but I know it is still vascular because when I become emotional it shows up.

My great-grandmother on my mother's side saw auras. Auras are the energy fields that surround every living organism. She assumed that everyone else saw them too. It wasn't until she was about eighteen years old that she discovered no one else she knew did, and so she decided to turn off this ability. She still saw the auras, but she did not process the incoming information that her gift provided. She chose to ignore her ability rather than develop it. Many people who have such abilities decide to conform to the norm rather than explore the unknown within themselves. I have often wondered how my great-grandmother's life would have been different had she accepted and developed this gift.

My dad has North American Indian blood on his mother's side. Her family belongs to the Penobscot Indian Nation, which is based in Maine. I have always enjoyed the idea of my Native heritage and its connection with nature and the universal energy. After doing some research, I discovered that I am related to the last-known Penobscot shaman healer, Sockalexis.

Although some shamans used their power to do harm to their enemies, Sockalexis was known to do only healings, and because of this he was highly respected and not feared by his fellow tribesmen. Shamans need to be humble and aware of their own strengths and weaknesses in order to help others. They must be able to use their skills and powers to adapt to any situation. This requires a balance of mind, body, heart and spirit. Healing must be an intuitive quest of learning about others and ourselves.

The meeting of these two spiritual worlds from my mother's side and my father's side formed my unconscious awareness and unknowingly led me along my path.

Many things that I see are not visible to most people. For example, I see auras. An aura appears to me as a luminous glow, which I see in various colors and patterns. People, animals and even plants have auras, which show that the living organism is functioning. Because of this ability to see auras, I had no trouble distinguishing reality from the fantasy world of television. I remember watching TV as a little kid and telling my mom and dad that there were "real" people and TV people. Auric fields of people and all life are lost during the transmission of television signals; hence, I saw people on TV as totally different from other people. That was helpful in determining the difference between real and make-believe.

My abilities to see auras also created some problems for me, as you can imagine. As a kid, I didn't enjoy playing hide-and-seek. It wasn't that I was antisocial or too shy. I just couldn't figure out the point of the game. Someone might be hiding behind a tree, but he was still visible to me: His aura showed beyond the tree's outline. It seemed as ludicrous as a large man trying to hide behind a broomstick. I didn't know that others weren't able to see the way I did. That was something I had to learn. Before I did, the point of such games mystified me.

Every time I went with my family into the wilderness, I spotted wildlife long before the others. For me, the animals' auras were visible through the brush or forest. Many times as our car traveled along a highway, my family couldn't see what I did. But often enough, the others eventually spotted it too, and my sightings were believed. It is human nature to believe only what we can see. I once read that "vision is the ability to see what isn't there." I see and feel the universal connectedness of all living things—human, animal and plant. I always have.

By the time I was in high school, I had learned to tone down the auras I saw. They were glaringly bright and had become obtrusive. Toning them down had an interesting result: My intuitiveness, or psychic ability, increased. Instead of "seeing" auras and interpreting them, I was able to pick up the information directly through intuition. I just "knew" things, as a sense of knowing. In high school, accepting and understanding this phenomenon was never encouraged nor even acknowledged.

Many people can see auras or were able to see them at one time in their lives. When I look at babies, I can tell that most are very aware of a person's aura. If I change mine (for instance, by projecting, through my thoughts and intention, it higher above my head), the baby's eyes will follow.

The seeing of auras is not nurtured in children mainly because most parents don't know their children have this ability. Some children are forced to suppress it, as the parents are fearful their child will be labeled mentally unstable. A family's religious belief might also pose a problem in accepting something like this. Doctors may want to prescribe drugs to "stop the hallucinations." Society has us thinking and believing that it is something that needs fixing.

Back in the 1600s, when people used their special abilities to heal, they were often called witches and burned at the stake. The leaders and scholars of the day would do their best to keep the public ignorant of what was really happening. They couldn't have been more wrong. Special abilities like mine need to be nurtured and understood in order to benefit all humankind.

But our thinking has a long way to go. For now, I know that what I experience is not understood and accepted. Rather, it is generally misunderstood and feared. I learned early in life that a regular kid in tennis shoes and a T-shirt had to keep quiet about being different.

Fortunately, my parents are rare and special spirits in that they came to accept my uniqueness. Even more, they came to realize my need for special guidance, or mentoring as it is sometimes called. They had the courage and the wisdom to allow me to be me. Within the context of a loving home environment and their open-mindedness, my gift has been allowed to grow and thrive. For this I will always be grateful. Because of my parents, I have a better chance of reaching my potential.

It couldn't have been easy for them. As I entered my teenage years and began to have telekinetic experiences, I was puzzled. I'm sure my parents were a little more than puzzled as well. Initially, they didn't believe me. Understandably, it was hard for them to accept it. It was especially difficult for my father, who looks for a scientific explanation for everything. It was easier for me because what was happening to me was my normal. I didn't know anything else.

Strange things seemed to always be happening to me. Objects often flew about the room when I went to touch them or pick them up. Sometimes the pencil I was writing with suddenly had a mind of its own and would take off across the room. This happened in school, and everyone figured I was throwing these objects. I let them think that. It was easier than telling them that they were trajected all on their own. I didn't know why or how this was happening, but I learned to live with it.

But the first time my bicycle did a 360-degree flip while I was riding it, I knew something was really different about me. My mom was with me when it happened, and she could hardly believe her eyes. I was glad she saw it. It is hard to keep overlooking happenings that you know are unusual. It's even harder when others discount them.

I tried to hide what was happening from the outside world, and was pretty successful at doing so. But it became impossible to hide it from my parents. We did a lot of activities together as a family, and they witnessed enough strange events that even my scientifically minded father could no longer deny it. He saw objects hit the ceiling with great force after I reached out to touch them.

The turning point for him, though, came one

day while we were at the gym working out. A forty-five-pound barbell fell off its rack near where I was standing and missed my dad's head by just inches. We thought the rack was faulty so we spent a great deal of time trying to duplicate the event, to no avail. There was nothing wrong with the equipment. It was then that my dad finally understood that unexplainable events were truly happening.

After that, his attitude changed and he became insatiably curious about my abilities. Both my parents became focused on how they could help me develop my gifts. Together, we began a journey.

Chapter 2
The Journey Begins

In the future, being able to heal
by thought will be the norm.

—ADAM

$\mathcal{M}$y dad is the type of guy you want to have around in an emergency. He's calm, level-headed and unflappable. He's the one who will take charge in a crisis and step right into action. But Dad became worried and concerned at the onset of accepting what was happening to me. Was this dangerous for me? Was it dangerous for others? There must be answers out there somewhere, but where?

In a panic, my mom phoned Grandma with an SOS. In normal circumstances, Grandma's advice was usually acted upon. It soon became apparent that this was not a typical childhood situation, or one she had any experience with. Her advice at first was to call a pediatrician. It didn't take long for all involved to realize that this was not the route to take. Then Mom remembered a woman she had met years ago. This woman had the ability to see auras and what she called external energy flow. Mom phoned with an urgent request for an appointment. Fresh from my episodes of pencil-flying and bike-flipping, we went to see her. We had no idea what to expect.

It was great. For the first time I totally connected to someone who could discuss what I had thought everyone could see and feel: energy flow. She showed me various pathways and patterns to redirect my energy in order to achieve different effects and emotions. What I was feeling was visible to her as well as to me.

She explained that the bike-flippings were outbursts of energy, like unintentional static electricity, that occurred when I was not focused on my energy flow. I have lots of energy that must be patterned properly. It was a great relief to hear that I could do no harm to others or myself. I think that she was correct, as the bike-flipping has not occurred since I began to direct my energy in other ways.

She told me to stretch my arms out to the side as far as I could. I was to send energy out of one hand and encircle the earth with it, receiving it in the other hand. It was wonderful to see this energy, which she called an aura. That was the first time that I had heard this word. It was so reassuring to know that others can see this energy. We were both totally immersed in changing the patterns of my aura.

Mom sat speechless throughout the session; it was all new territory for her. But it was definitely not new for me. I understood with total clarity what was happening. I was finally able to control my energy. This came as a great relief to me, as well as to my parents. Having a sane adult describe what was happening helped us all understand that this was the normal state for me. Her parting words to my mom and me were that we should look into Qigong (pronounced "chee gong"). "Qi," sometimes spelled chi, means energy or life force. "Gong" means discipline or work.

"With the amount of energy he has, he could be a Grandmaster in a week," the woman told my parents. I've since learned that it often takes decades of dedicated study to reach that level.

As suggested, I made an appointment with a Qigong Master in town. It was interesting to watch as he demonstrated emitting chi, which was streaming out of his body through his fingertips. What an experience it was to be able to see this! He had a large, golden aura that seemed to flow harmoniously. I was curious and wanted to learn more about energy systems.

This encounter was a turning point for me. I had discovered that I could control and focus my energy. I wasn't flirting with madness but, rather, exploring a gift that others shared. From here, I embarked on the self-discovery part of my journey.

HEALING DISCOVERY

Two days after my meeting with the Qigong Master, my mom was in severe pain from trigeminal neuralgia, a stabbing pain in the face and ear that is caused, in my mom's case, by her multiple sclerosis

(MS), a neurological disease. She had been diagnosed with MS when I was very young, and so this was not a new experience for any of us in the family.

That particular night, my dad, my sister and I were watching television and Mom was upstairs in her bedroom smothering her screams in her pillow. At times like this, we felt helpless to relieve her of her pain, and Mom preferred to be by herself. The pain was, as it was on many nights, unbearable. Finally, I went up to her room.

"Close your eyes, Mom," I said to her as I put my hands on her head. Why I did this I really don't know. It's as though I knew what to do. She complied, and I felt the pain leave her body and enter mine. It was a horrible pain.

I went to my bed and collapsed on it with a throbbing headache. My mom drifted off to sleep, pain-free. She has improved a great deal since that night and we are now able to do more things together as a family.

This was yet another turning point for me in understanding my gifts. It sealed my journey toward healing. Everything seems to evolve for a reason, and my mom's illness was no exception. This was no coincidence but a signpost. It allowed me to start my healing journey from a point of no fear, with the intention only of helping my mom.

If it weren't for my mom's illness, I likely wouldn't have dived headfirst into healing; rather, it would probably have been something I gradually came to years later. Seeing someone whom I love suffer was the inspiration I needed to react without thoughts of whether I could or couldn't help, of whether this was even possible. As if on autopilot, I did what I could do and made another self-discovery—I could heal.

But another challenge emerged for us. I had absorbed her pain and taken it on as my own. Once again, my parents were concerned. They certainly didn't want me healing if I was going to be ill as a result. Nevertheless, I was instinctively drawn to healing. While driving with my parents, I often noted injuries and medical conditions of the people we passed.

I recall sitting in a doctor's waiting room with

my dad. Four other kids—one just a baby—were sitting across from us with their parents. This ability of mine to see auras is always on, so my attention was instinctively drawn to reading the kids' auras. Of course, they were unaware of what I was doing. I could clearly see that the aura surrounding the baby's lungs was alight with a problem. I felt upset that I couldn't say anything to the doctor about this, as the baby was unable to explain her symptoms.

Healing and health became a predominant theme in my life. Initially, I did some treatments on people from my dad's workplace. These people were socially separate from any of my high school friends or neighbors, so I didn't feel threatened by their knowing of my unusual abilities. Most were about my dad's age and typically dealing with old sports injuries and pain issues. One fellow had hurt his neck fifteen years earlier in a skiing accident. Even turning his head while driving was challenging for him. After one treatment, his range of neck mobility returned to near normal and his chronic pain disappeared. Word gradually got around the office, and I was kept quite busy. During this time, I learned a lot through practice.

But my parents were still not confident enough to be relaxed about my healing experiences. They wondered about the possibilities of my picking up some serious disease as I learned and practiced new techniques. After many sleepless nights, they called Dr. Effie Chow, a Qigong Grandmaster.

Mom met Dr. Chow years earlier at a Qigong demonstration. Dr. Chow is founder and president of the East West Academy of Healing Arts, in San Francisco. In July 2000, U.S. president Bill Clinton appointed Dr. Chow to the original fifteen-member White House Commission on Complementary and Alternative Medicine Policy. Dr. Chow has a Ph.D. in higher education and a master's degree in behavioral sciences and communications. She is a registered public health and psychiatric nurse, an acupuncturist and a Qigong Grandmaster with thirty-five years of experience.

Even with her qualifications and busy schedule, she managed to find time to come to our city and mentor me for three days. My time with her was further how interconnected we really are, as I was able to see by way of our connecting auras the energy that others could feel. Changing the energy field of one person affected all persons in or near that energy field. If someone is in a negative mood, all people around him will have a tendency to feel negative. If you are around someone who is positive, you will tend to be in a positive mood.

One of the most important techniques I learned from Dr. Chow was visualization. When I first met Dr. Chow, I had limited experience in removing people's energy blockages. She taught me how to visualize different tools for removing energy blocks, and I was able to be more effective with my healings. For example, when I first looked at someone with multiple sclerosis, the disease looked like grains of green sand. My usual approach was to envision picking up each grain and throwing it away. I found this technique extremely inefficient, as the blockages returned as fast as I could remove them. When I described to Dr. Chow what I was doing, she told me a more efficient visualization method for this. I found that it was more efficient to visualize the vacuuming up of these grains of sand and then the disposing of these energy blockages.

I learned that imagination is the most powerful tool in healing. This realization allowed me to actively participate in my own healing evolution. I became self-confident enough to learn by experience rather than depending on acquired skills from others. I began to experiment and learn what worked the most effectively for me. Some day, being able to heal by thought and imagination will be the norm. There are no limits in this new healing reality.

Chapter 3
Finding My Way

Every person is born with gifts.
Life itself is the most precious of them.

—ADAM

$\mathcal{A}$ journey is a sequence of events. It begins with the first step, which in my case was the recognition that I was different. I believe it is the responsibility of all of us to use the gifts with which we are born. I choose to use mine for the benefit of others. It would be a shame to ignore them and deprive others of this knowledge and benefit.

Life is one of the most precious gifts. Life gives one the connection to what I call the universal energy field. The science of quantum physics refers to this as the field of quantum information. Awareness of this connection is in itself a gift.

People's gifts and talents vary. My younger sister

has the gift of a musical ear. Wherever she goes, she hears music. Whether she is in a shopping mall or in the wilderness, she is tuned in to it. She can't ignore her musical ear or turn it off. It is one of her gifts.

Similarly, visual artists must see a potential painting everywhere they look. Everyone can appreciate the incredible beauty of a rock-faced canyon with a river roaring through it toward the open ocean. Evergreens line the bluffs and their scent permeates our thoughts. Strong gusts of wind energize us as we feel our connectedness to the universal energy field, which engulfs us, connects us and is us. We can feel the oneness with all, but it takes an artist to see the emerging work of art; it is the artists who try to capture that feeling on canvas with their gifts.

Others are gifted with athleticism and are able to move with incredible agility or remarkable speed. They excel in mind–body coordination. All gifts are important. We are interdependent on each other's contributions, and no gift is any more or any less important than any other gift.

One of my gifts is being sensitive to our

connectedness with the universal energy and each other. This connection goes by many names, but whatever it is called, it is a connection we all share. Calling it the universal energy field is perhaps most straightforward. Some people might refer to it by saying, "May the force be with you," but this is not really accurate, as the force is always with you. Some people are aware of it, and others are not, but it is there nonetheless.

So many things happen in life that one passes off as just coincidence. From some of my experiences, I have begun to think differently on this topic. Have you ever heard yourself say, "I knew that was going to happen"? Many of us have experienced this. We receive information from the universal information field constantly. It is just a matter of screening out what you don't need and making sense of what is useful. We must be aware of these coincidences and cultivate their messages and meaning. Most coincidences are messages that are sent for a reason. That reason may have to do with you. Or it might be intended for someone with whom you will be in contact—perhaps you are being used as a conduit for another person in need.

All information past and present is out there and available to us. The universal energy field is exactly that: universal. All inventions, medical cures and knowledge come from the universal energy field. Sometimes we access great ideas and surprise ourselves. The human ego being what it is, you might be tempted to assume you are very smart to have come up with the idea. There is nothing wrong with thinking highly of yourself. But you did not come upon this great idea solely through your own thought. You were assisted by many people who have their ideas filed in the universal energy field. We all share our thoughts and ideas in this way. And sometimes, it is accessed simultaneously. The refrigerator, for example, was invented at the same time by two different men in two different countries. They were never in touch with each other, but each accessed the necessary information at the same time.

A friend of my mom's is a talented graphic designer, and many of her clients and associates are in awe of her work. They frequently ask her how she comes up with her amazing designs, and some are disappointed with her answer. "I honestly don't know how I am able to create these results," she says. "But I don't feel as though they come *from* me. I feel as though they come *through* me."

I know what she means, and I appreciate her awareness. But it is often hard for those around her to accept it. They think that perhaps she has a self-esteem issue. I think she is simply aware of her connection to the universal energy field and routinely taps into it during her creative process, just as I tap into the universal energy field to do my healing.

Healing is something I can't ignore. This ability is not coincidental. It was given to me for a reason, and I plan to use it. I am still in high school and involved in regular social and sport activities. However, being able to remove illness from people is very rewarding. I just wish that I had more time to treat everyone who needs it, as well as play basketball, tennis, snowboard, chat with my girlfriend and just generally hang out with my friends. I am a regular sixteen-year-old … sort of.

Because of my gift of sensitivity to universal connectedness, I am able to heal. I think I always knew I could heal, but thought I needed to hide the ability from others. I would be alienated or rejected if I exposed this gift to those around me. Many other people who have unusual abilities feel they must choose between a social life and living with their uniqueness. I choose both, although integrating them is still very challenging for me. My social life is important to me. But so is the ability to share my healing gifts, so I must constantly balance the two.

I have had the privilege of working with other healers in many disciplines, such as Qigong and Reiki. Although what I do is based on what I experience, I found there was always something new to learn that I could incorporate into what I do. For instance, when I first began healing, I found it very draining, as I took the energy blockage out of the person I was healing by drawing it into me. So one of the things I had to learn was to heal in a way that didn't harm me. As I said earlier, that was important to my ever vigilant parents. My mom is especially watchful that I do not overextend myself and that I get enough rest. This meant I had to find a way to heal without taking on the other person's pain. So with some coaching from experts in the healing arts, and over time, I fine-tuned my own techniques.

My first step to understanding energy was to know that seeing auras or human energy fields is rare but certainly not unique to me. I soon realized that this ability is a gift, and I learned that I can control it. It can also be redirected and connected with any other life energy fields, including that of all humans, animals and plant life. This energy field connection could be used for healing. Many times I felt I was in uncharted territory as I explored this new gift. I have developed my own methods and style of healing through self-teaching. But that is not to say that I have not had input along the way.

The energy healing I do is not Reiki (Japanese healing art), Qigong, touch therapy or faith healing. It falls under no particular discipline. My ability to heal is what comes naturally to me. I wanted to learn what other healers do so I met with many of them. With my ability to see auras, it is obvious to me what is happening as I can see the energy flow from healer to patient. What is invisible to most people, including many healers, is clearly visible to me.

One of the first healers I met showed me how to ground my energy, something Dr. Chow had told me about. Grounding is connecting one's life energy to the earth's energy. He explained that with exhaling, I should imagine the flow of my energy traveling down my body, through the soles of my feet, all the way to the center of the earth. This knowledge of grounding energy is essential to everyone. We connect to the universal energy field with each inhale—by breathing in and absorbing it. This completes the energy circuit, and we ground. I was thrilled with this knowledge and now my energy flows smoothly.

Another mentor I met with is a Reiki psychic healer, and I learned something of this type of healing. I engaged in telepathic communication or mind talk with this healer. To be able to do this was a first for me. We sat in the same room and had conversations without exchanging any words. Instead, we communicated by exchanging mental images. I enjoyed this form of communication, as it is so efficient compared with verbal communication.

Much of the information received from hearing someone speak is based on the receiver's interpretation of what was intended. Interpretations may vary widely from the speaker's original meaning. Communication through the use of mental imaging conveys a more direct meaning: A picture really is worth a thousand words.

Later I met another healer who also communicated to me with images. He had healed himself of terminal cancer and uses the knowledge he gained from this experience to help others. He works by increasing the vibrational level of the body. From him I learned about the vibrational levels of various colors and how this affects healing. Our bodies are tuned in to so many more aspects of the universe than we might think.

I also had the pleasure of meeting a local healer who discovered his healing ability by accident. Many years ago, he was first on the scene after someone was injured. He instinctively held his hands over the injury. Heat radiated from them and the person immediately noticed that his pain disappeared. Both the healer and the injured man were shocked by what happened. For fear of being ostracized, the healer tried to forget this event. He spent most of his life working in a high-tech field, trying to avoid his connection to healing. Of course, he found that he had to use his gift. It would wait until he was ready to use it, but it would not go away.

I found that each healer's strengths are different, and I have incorporated into my healings a technique or idea from most I have met. From all, I learned something valuable: We are all in this together, working toward the greater good.

Initially, I met people engaged in the healing arts who focus on the outer energy area of a person's body, or the aura. Healers use their hands and minds to smooth and repair the energy blockages negatively affecting the body. Many healers have found this to be an effective technique for dealing with health problems. Auras are an easy place to first notice illness or injury, as they are extensions and reflections of the body. Illness or injury prominently shows in one's energy field, leading the healer to the location of the problem. Various colors given off by this energy within the auric field provide lots of information.

The color is not the only visible indicator of trouble. I find that the entire aura of the injured or diseased part of the body is disturbed. In healthy areas of the body, the aura moves and swirls in a pattern and appears organized and in harmony. There is a flow. In an afflicted area, this flow is broken. The appearance is definitely that of disharmony.

My vision goes much deeper than the aura of energy, which surrounds all living things. I have the ability to see energy fields, at many different frequencies, which enables me to do a type of body scan on a person. Dr. Effie Chow, in her book *Miracle Healing from China,* mentions this as a rare ability of a few Qigong Masters. It is sometimes referred to as X-ray vision.

It is possible for me to see these blockages or disruptions even before the person feels it, if it is a new blockage being created. When it is new, the

Chapter 4

The Science Behind It All

It will take the devotion of many
to awaken mankind to our connectivity.

—ADAM

$\mathcal{M}$y dad has always said that there is a scientific explanation for everything. In our society, anything that we can't explain with our scientific knowledge is called a mystery. If something very good occurs and we can't explain how it happened, we call it a miracle. Doctors sometimes have patients whom they predict will live only a few months and to their surprise go on to live for years. The doctors refer to this as a miracle simply because the understanding of what took place is beyond their medical knowledge.

Many of the pioneers of science have been ridiculed for delving into that which was not in line with the scientific views of the day. I have had the honor of meeting a modern-day scientist who has no fear of exploring what he strongly believes. His name is Dr. Edgar Mitchell. His name will no doubt be familiar to many readers. On January 31, 1971, *Apollo 14* lifted off from Cape Kennedy (now Cape Canaveral) and three days later, Edgar Mitchell and Alan Shepard walked on the lunar surface. As could be expected from such a dramatic and meaningful experience, Dr. Mitchell's perspective on life and human consciousness was never the same again. A graduate of Cambridge's Massachusetts Institute of Technology, with a doctorate in aeronautics and astronautics, Dr. Mitchell has since constructed a theory that could explain not only the mystery of human consciousness but the psychic event as well. It is my opinion that Dr. Mitchell is one of the great thinkers of our time.

On Dr. Mitchell's return journey to earth, he became aware of a deep sense of universal connectedness. This overwhelming awareness set the course for him in years to come. For the next thirty-plus years, he studied the mysteries of consciousness and being. For years, Dr. Edgar Mitchell has studied the quantum hologram, which puts an important scientific description to human phenomena, including consciousness itself. The scientific papers he has written are complex and go beyond what I would like to cover in this book. Nevertheless, his ability to explain things to me in scientific terms has helped me understand my gift and progress with it.

"Magic," "miracles" and "natural phenomena" are labels we give to things we can't understand with our existing knowledge. When people refer to any healing I do as a miracle, I correct them. Everything I do has a scientific basis; we just have to discover it. Dr. Edgar Mitchell's paper entitled *Nature's Mind— The Quantum Hologram* comes closest to explaining what is happening when I connect to someone's energy field. It is always encouraging to come back to Dr. Mitchell for an explanation of any changes in what I am doing. He has been gracious and patient while helping me with my journey through this unusual time in my life. His mentoring has been invaluable to my understanding of the scientific meaning behind my ability.

DREAMHEALER

I believe also that there is no such thing as random coincidences. Things happen for a reason, and I feel that my meeting Dr. Mitchell was an essential part of my development. The chain of coincidences started with my uncle, whose hobby is manned space travel. His house is full of model rockets and spacecraft. He also has most books ever written by astronauts, including Dr. Edgar Mitchell's *The Way of the Explorer*.

My uncle came to our house one day with a pamphlet advertising a conference entitled *Quickening Global Consciousness*. This was the first time I heard about the Institute of Noetic Sciences or IONS, the organization Dr. Mitchell founded thirty years ago. Among many other issues, it explores distant healing. This information came to me at the exact moment I needed it. Had this happened even a month before, I don't think I would have been ready for it.

My parents and I arrived for the conference early and found seats near the front. There were two extra chairs at our table and several empty tables at the back. There were about two hundred people in the audience. Just before the guest speaker was introduced, a friend of Dr. Mitchell's joined us, though we didn't realize her connection with him until we began chatting during the intermission. I was still uncomfortable with people knowing about my healing gift and had decided before arriving at the conference that I wouldn't reveal why I had come. Nevertheless, when she asked why I was there—I was the youngest attendee by twenty-five years or so—I decided to tell her that I have healing abilities. Dr. Mitchell's friend had recently been in an accident and was interested in me seeing the injuries.

When I looked at her, I could see that her neck and back were painful to her. I also noted a sharp foreign object in a spot on her neck. When I told her this, she was astounded. The previous week, her doctor had injected a painkiller into her neck in an attempt to lessen her pain. Unbeknownst to the doctor, the tip of the needle had broken off. An X-ray revealed that it was located where I saw what looked like a sharp object. She was so taken by what I told her that she immediately decided to introduce us to Dr. Mitchell.

Since then, I have appreciated the knowledge, guidance and insight Dr. Mitchell and IONS has offered me. It is reassuring to meet intelligent people who want to explore and understand the unknown. The world would not have advanced to where it is today if it weren't for people like Dr. Edgar Mitchell.

And people such as physicist Max Planck. Just over a hundred years ago, Mr. Planck wrote a mathematical formula that introduced the world to the concept of tiny bundles of energy that behave both as waves and as particles. They came to be known as quanta. His formula became the basis of quantum physics and gave birth to a branch of science in which reality does not follow the cause-and-effect rules of empirical science. This changed our most basic concept of our physical world.

Humans do not welcome change. There is great resistance to it in many aspects of life. Many people were shocked when it was first proposed that the world is round, not flat. Most people were determined to reject the concept.

Indeed, the Flat Earth Society of the time was adamant that anyone who believed the world was round had lost his mind. Within the scholarly community, it didn't matter how many people you asked—you got the same response. They all shared the same thought, theory and answers. Hundreds of years later, we readily accept that the earth is round and think that those who fought so hard to hold on to the belief and doctrine that the world was flat were out of *their* minds.

It is not uncommon for new concepts to be viewed initially with suspicion. There is a reluctance to accept change. This is true of any science of the day, including medical science. At any particular place or time in history, whether you ask one or ten doctors a particular question, the answer is based on the same body of knowledge—though the answer itself is, of course, not always the same. For instance, several hundred years ago it was common practice for doctors to bleed their patients, which was often considered a necessary procedure. Anyone who suggested anything different at that time was viewed with distrust. Today, doctors use surgery, radiation and toxic drugs to treat cancer and other diseases. Over time, many of these treatments and procedures will become obsolete. I am fortunate in that I am not restricted by the dogma of the day as to what is possible or impossible. Nevertheless, the scientific explanations of how I perceive life energies, or auras, became important in my understanding of what I saw and did. Validating these experiences was important to me.

Soon after I realized that I could see and influence these subtle energies, I discovered that all I needed was a photograph of someone to be able to see that person's body scan remotely. This is the technique I use when doing distant healings. It enables me to treat anyone anywhere in the world. The distance between us does not matter. A connection is made using this universal stream of information so I don't need to be physically near someone to heal her. We are all connected.

I have found that understanding some of the basic principles of quantum theory is necessary in understanding how distant healing is possible. The nature of reality in the quantum world is a giant leap from that of our everyday material world. For example, a quantum object (such as an electron) can be at more than one place at a time. It does not exist in ordinary space-time reality until we observe it as a particle. A quantum particle ceases to exist in one place, only to simultaneously appear in another, and yet we cannot say that it traveled through the intervening space. This is referred to as a quantum leap. The most important concept that relates distant healing to quantum physics is nonlocality, or quantum action-at-a-distance. A quantum object simultaneously influences its correlated twin object, no matter how far apart they are. This explains how energy can influence other energy elsewhere.

All particles are fundamentally connected to each other. All information and knowledge is available in the field of quantum information. Every physical object emits its own quantum hologram, or image, whether it is on this planet or on a planet located on the other side of the universe. My visual perception of the field of quantum information looks amazingly similar to what I see in a person's brain. When I see the inside of the brain at an energetic level, I see synapses clicking on and off at an astonishing rate through a network of pathways that connect every neuron in the brain. Each node in the field of quantum information I am viewing is a bright, dense light that looks a bit like a spider cocoon. Each cocoon has zillions of pathways that stretch out, each attaching to another cocoon. This pattern seems to continue infinitely.

The following words from the Vedas, collections of sacred writings of ancient India, are over seven thousand years old. It is interesting to me how they match my visualization of the universal energy field, or field of quantum information. The jeweled net of Indra—Indra was the supreme ruler of the gods in Vedic times—is a perfect example of how every point reflects to every other point. Interconnectedness and interdependency of everyone and everything in the universe is similar to the holographic view. Both the materialistic world of the jewels themselves and the nonmaterial world of energy as reflections of light exist as inseparable parts of the whole.

Indra's Net

There is an endless net of threads throughout the universe.

The horizontal threads are in space.
The vertical threads in time. At every crossing of
threads there is an individual.
And every individual is a crystal bead.
The great light of absolute being illuminates and
penetrates every crystal being,

And every crystal being reflects not only the light
from every other crystal in the net,
But also every reflection of every reflection
throughout the universe.

A person who is intuitive and energetically powerful can access this field and query it to find any information whatsoever. When an intuitive individual connects to another person, the information is received instantaneously because of this interconnectedness. The description of Indra's Net puts this complex concept into simple words.

The most important part of the quantum hologram that relates to my healing gift is that quantum attribute of nature called nonlocality. At the quantum level, action on two particles, which are part of a single system, occur instantaneously at a distance. It doesn't matter how far apart they are. This gives me a better understanding of how I am able to heal someone from a distance. I connect to a person's quantum hologram, which is a nonlocal information mechanism. I am then able to give information to the person's body through intentionality—my intention to heal—which causes the energy blockages to clear and allows energy to flow harmoniously and, thus, the body to change. The person's new state of wellness will then be emitted in the quantum hologram. With my intent to heal and the person's desire to get better, this can turn into real, positive results. I discuss this in more detail below, in "How I Heal."

In the last century, the early adapters of quantum principles have produced advanced technologies such as lasers, transistors and CT scanners. But in many areas, including our everyday lives, it is difficult for most people to think in terms of the quantum phenomenon. When we go to work each day, we like to know that our office is exactly where it was when we left it yesterday. It would be difficult for architects and engineers who are busy designing and building skyscrapers and bridges to think in terms of something existing in two places at once. It is not an easy reach, to say the least. But I believe that, over time, we will unravel the mysteries of this most interesting form of science and learn to apply the principles and concepts in many areas, to enormous benefit.

HOW I HEAL

I have been asked many times what I see, experience and know when I do a healing. When I first started healing, the person would be seated next to me while my arm and hand was outstretched toward her. This enabled my energy system to interact with hers. Now distance is not a barrier. It makes no difference if the person is sitting next to me or on the other side of the world. When I see a photograph of the person, I can instantly connect to her energy system.

Every physical object emits its own quantum hologram, which contains all information about it. From this field of quantum information, I can zoom in on specific information or views, which I project as holographic images in front of me when I am viewing someone for treatment. These holograms are the visual guidance, or three-dimensional maps. All the body's information is available in this manner. I discuss my use of holograms in more detail in the next chapter.

Once a hologram appears, I can manipulate the energy so that the person can find her way back to a healthy state. People who have observed me doing this tell me that it looks as though I am conducting an orchestra. My arms and hands wave through the air, and my fingers nimbly create patterns as I make energy adjustments. To the observer, I appear to be making mesmerizing yet patterned flowing gestures, like the dancing of flames in a raging fire. Through my intentions of healing, I provide information to the person I am treating. I do this by being in resonance with the person's body. This means that the frequency that we are tuned to is similar. In this way, the body of the person is interacting and exchanging information with me. This then stimulates the person to energetically alter her state of wellness, which is in turn reflected in the hologram. I can usually see this change starting to take place immediately.

Everyone's body knows its own way back to wellness—it just needs some guidance. These adjustments to the person's energy system help the body achieve this. I have done energy adjustments hundreds of times, yet my parents want to watch each time. Mom says that she can feel a tingly sensation every time I do an energy treatment.

As I developed and practiced my techniques, I found a way to dispose of the pain of the person I was treating, rather than taking it on. Now I send it to a black hole of sorts. I don't destroy it; it just seems to die on its own without the host organism (the person's body).

I had to learn to use the universal energy that flows through a person rather than using the energy that flows through me. This is more efficient because all healing is really done by the person herself, when she energetically alters her state of wellness. I have discovered that using the universal energy field is a far more efficient and powerful

method of healing. This seemingly endless source of
energy is much more efficient to use than using a
person's own energy to heal. Every person knows
where this universal energy is needed in the body in
order to heal herself.

The following poem explains the relationship
between healing and learning. The only true connection to knowledge and healing is that which we
learn for ourselves.

Learning *can only be done by oneself.*
Nobody else *can learn anything for us.*
Healing *can only be accomplished by oneself.*
Nobody else *can heal for us.*
Teachers *can mentor us, direct us to informa-
tion,*
Encourage and assist us in the process.
Healers *can help us connect to our own energy
sources, give us hope and guidance.*
When we are ready we will learn *the knowledge
ourselves.*
When we are ready we will heal *our bodies our-
selves.*

Our minds will learn, *and*
Our bodies will heal
Only when we are ready

—Adam

How did you know when you were able to start doing distant healings?

I always trust that when I am ready for more information, it will come. At that time I had a need to refine and develop my techniques as my outstretched arm that I used for healing became incredibly strained. My dad asked me to move farther away from the person and see if I could still connect effectively to the information that I "see." I soon found that if I was in the next room, the connection was just the same. Shortly after this, I was shown photographs of people and I was amazed that all of the data I received were just as clear to me as if that person were right beside me. We experimented with photographs of people in town and of people around the world. The information was just as precise, and so we discovered that distance is not a factor.

How are you able to prevent taking on the pain of the person you are healing?

Energy moves by intention. Through the intention of disposing of energy blockages, it is done. I have a clear image in my mind as to how I will do this; for example, launching it into black holes, or vacuuming it up and then throwing it in the garbage.

The ancient poem of "Indra's Net" seems very mystical. How is it related to modern-day life?

In spite of our technological advances, we still live within our connection to everything else in our universe. We affect and are affected by the entire net, as described in the poem. In this way, each and every one of us *is* the entire web of existence. Regardless of any scientific advances, our interconnectivity is the most fundamental law of the universe.

Chapter 5
Holograms and Colors

Through my intentions to heal, I can send new information to the person, allowing him or her to change to a new state of health.

—ADAM

I first started healing by using the overall energy holographic projections, or holograms, which shows energy blockages. I am constantly evolving new techniques and holographic layers for the new challenges I meet in healing.

USING HOLOGRAMS

When I first started healing, I saw and worked with one hologram to see, identify and clear energy blockages. I could do a virtual tour of the inside of someone's body with what appeared to me to be a still photo of all the organs and inner structure of the body. Energy blockages appeared prominently in the foreground, so I was able to easily see and remove them. I often found this work tiring and sometimes had a headache afterward. When I am working with a hologram, I lose all sense of time. I also had to be careful to remember to breathe rather than hold my breath. The breathing now comes naturally to me, but it was certainly part of the learning process. I definitely had much to discover about my techniques.

One day I was looking at a young man with a heart problem. All of a sudden, I found myself inside his body in real time. I was surrounded by the beating heart, pulsating blood, contracting arteries and moving valves. I couldn't escape this overwhelming realistic view. Graphic images surrounded me. I stepped back in awe and total shock of what I was experiencing. Believe me, it wasn't a pretty sight. I released myself during my step backwards and, once out, I felt ill, dizzy and exhausted. I had to go to bed immediately to sleep it off.

Since that experience, I have learned how to go in and out of this holographic view of one's body and remain in control, rather than letting it control me. I have a total sense of being there, and I can watch the entire body in action from the inside. I take a visual tour of the body of the person I am treating, *from the inside*. I can see every organ as it is functioning, or struggling to function. I see and hear the heart pumping. I watch cancer grow. I watch the traffic of synapses in the brain. Every cell and every activity can be visible to me as I go through the treatment. I call it "going in." I don't do this all the time. Usually I go into the energetic hologram, doing this physical real-time hologram only if it is needed for a specific problem.

When I go into someone, I can tune in to various subsets of information. It's kind of like changing channels on the TV. My mind acts as the remote control, which can adjust to different sets of frequencies, thus giving me different holographic views: I project a subset of information as a holographic image in front of me, and I am able to zoom in and out as required, as if I were using a microscope. I choose the hologram most useful for the ailment I am treating. The following are the seven holographic views I use most frequently, but I am sure I'll be using more as soon as I develop them.

Energetic Hologram

This is the first hologram I learned to use. It is at the most basic level and for many simple ailments it is the most effective. With it, I can see an overall view of the energetic body. The body's energy system grid shows the flow of energy, as well as any blockages, old or new. Energy changes provide a grid-type guide for a person's body to model for the path to healing: Reminding the body of its healthy state is often all that is needed. Through my intentions to heal, I can give new information to that person's body, which allows it to change to its new state of health.

If something is removed on the energetic level, it will soon disappear on the physical level. A woman I treated had been bleeding vaginally. Her gynecologist had ordered an ultrasound of her uterus, which showed a fibroid mass, or polyp. Surgery to remove it was scheduled.

I went in and had no trouble locating the bleeding area. It was a very small polyp that was causing the problem. I removed it energetically and saw that the woman's body was adjusting to the change. In her hologram, it looked as though her body would continue to heal itself. Six weeks later, when the surgery was performed, the gynecologist was amazed to find that there was no polyp. He later told the woman that he didn't understand how this could be but that "the case is closed," and if she had bleeding again, it was unrelated.

The energetic view is also the one I use to treat sports-related injuries. These types of injuries are often readily visible as a blockage and it is usually uncomplicated to manipulate the energy flow.

Brain Signals Hologram

In this hologram I can see the flow of electrical impulses along neurons and intuitively know their function. I can see damaged connections that are specific to certain brain functions. All the switches in the brain allow or prevent the passage of electrical impulses. The flow and blockages of these electrical pathways form a specialized holographic view of the brain. Any brain disease or injury shows up in the hologram as an area that brain signals do not readily and efficiently travel through. This area is the energy blockage, causing all signaling to reroute itself. The brain signals hologram is a useful tool for healing headaches, migraines and neurological disorders. For certain recurring problems, the brain needs to be reset.

Viewing the brain signals hologram in real time is like being in the middle of a three-dimensional superhighway. There are electrical impulses flying along pathways everywhere, and I do mean flying. The speed at which they travel is incredible. It took some practice until I felt comfortable viewing this hologram.

A woman I know was misdiagnosed many years ago as having MS. This was before the current diagnostic tests were available. Recently, she had an MRI and was told she does not have MS. Rather, her cerebellum has simply stopped functioning. She has great difficulty with mobility (she had to use a walker), which contributed to the MS misdiagnosis.

Her neurologist could not establish what caused her condition but said that it did not appear to be progressive.

When I first went in, I could see right away that part of her brain had no functioning neurons. I used her brain signals hologram to get the flow of energy going in this area. After a few sessions, I could see an energetic difference as new pathways began to develop. The woman, however, felt no change but thanked me for my efforts.

Several months after our sessions, I heard from her. She had noticed a gradual but marked improvement in her mobility and coordination. The physical improvement *did* follow the energetic strides I saw. Her body just took some time to react.

Real-Time Physical Hologram

The real-time physical hologram involves the nervous, musculoskeletal and energetic systems, as well as the organs. I can see any of these at a cellular level, if need be, and adjust it to its best healing potential. I like to use this hologram to observe the functioning of different body systems.

From here, I can determine the next course of action.

This hologram is particularly useful when the person I am treating has a musculoskeletal disorder such as fibromyalgia or rheumatoid arthritis.

Smart Energy Packets

Through intentionality, I send these Pacman-like units into the body's information to reduce the unwanted blockages and replace them with good energy. I call them smart energy packets (SEPs).

SEPs are an extremely useful healing tool for me. It is a tool that I use to eliminate things on an energetic level that would require ongoing work, as SEPs can continue to heal long after my treatment is finished. I use SEPs on infections, cancer and other such problems that have a great potential to reoccur.

SEPs are more than a "seek and destroy" device. They have a sack on them that spreads good healing energy along their path. They can also reproduce themselves and communicate with each other, sending signals to each other to shock or jumpstart the system. I am constantly developing more efficient and effective SEPs.

Pattern Energy Grid

The pattern energy grid can reveal if there is a dysfunction or disease occurring because the source of the problem stubbornly remains. When I look at three-dimensional contour maps, I can quickly tell if there is an imperfection in the graph. In a similar way, I detect dysfunction or disease in the pattern energy grid. There is harmony and flow in the hologram of a healthy system, and a disruption around the dysfunction is clearly visible as energy reroutes itself around blockages. Old, stubborn injuries appear prominently in the pattern energy grid hologram. New injuries are not as pronounced. This view is not of the external aura but of much deeper energy patterns in the body.

If the body recognizes its healthy state, the deviation will also be recognized and dealt with by the body's immune system. The pattern energy grid is also useful after a treatment to hold the new energy pattern in place.

Heat Hologram

I have found this hologram useful in my treatment of cancer. Every visualization has variations, including different ways of applying heat. The only limitation on the number of applications is imagination. To me, cancer cells appear as green. After red heat is energetically applied, these cells gradually turn white and disintegrate like dust. Then I energetically vacuum up the dead bits. A variation is energetic red heat, or high-frequency energy, which can be used to pop cancer cells from the inside out. They explode on the energetic level and die. If something is dead on the energetic level, it usually dies on the physical level shortly after.

Overall-View Hologram

I compare how this hologram looks before and after each treatment to see if the person has accepted the new pattern of health. If energy blockages have been removed, that should appear obvious to me. Some people and some conditions appear to shift toward health in one treatment. Others take more treatments and time—the effectiveness of a treatment varies with each person. This overall view is how I know what impact the treatments have had and whether more treatments are needed.

Genetic Hologram

This is my eighth and newest holographic image. Genetic diseases are complicated, as the body sees the defect as part of its rightful and healthy state. I'm not yet ready to use this view. But I know there are many applications within the information contained in this hologram, and I will continue researching it so I can fully understand its potential.

USING COLORS

Each color has its own energy frequency. Colors are applicable to any hologram for healing. I know that there have been many suggestions as to what each color means and how it can be used for manipulating moods and even healing. I have simply observed colors, their vibrations and their effects. Over time, I have figured out how they work by watching auras and studying energy fields. I watch how auras look and move when people are sick and when they are healthy. That is how I have come to know which color to use, and when.

I have been asked if the average person can help himself or someone else by visualizing the appropriate color around him or around the afflicted area. My answer is that it depends on the person. Most people who are willing to discipline themselves and learn to focus can use colors to help themselves and others. Everyone has the ability to heal to some degree. The "Seven Steps for Life" section of this book outlines how everyone can maximize this capability.

If you break anything in the universe down to its basics, you have energy. Light is the visible frequency range of the electromagnetic energy spectrum. There are many other frequency ranges that we cannot perceive with our five senses, yet we know they exist. If we are exposed to large doses of electromagnetic waves in the upper frequencies, such as ultraviolet, X-rays, gamma rays or cosmic rays, we will eventually die from this exposure. It is no surprise that cancer will also die from exposure to high-frequency electromagnetic waves. This technique is used in a number of medical technologies to kill cancer. The problem is that this often kills the normal cells surrounding the cancer, causing serious side effects.

One of the methods I use to treat diseases is applying high energy directly to the diseased area, without damaging normal cells. The only side effect is from the body adjusting to a new, and therefore unfamiliar, healthy state. I see the energy that I apply in the form of colors inside the body. During this process I am able to access colors outside the standard spectrum, colors I can see only in my mind. These are of a much higher frequency and are extremely useful in healing. These colors are impossible to describe. It's like asking someone who can see only the color green to describe the color red.

The concentration of a certain color of light is made denser when it is focused like a laser beam. This makes it more effective for healing small areas. There are so many combinations of colors and densities that it is impossible for me to summarize all the different results at this stage in my discovery. Some combinations of colors are synergistic. White and purple, for example, work well together. Here are brief descriptions of the colors within the standard spectrum that I use most frequently.

Yellow: Yellow is used when an organ or localized area requires treatment. It is used to increase energy when someone suffers from a lack of it. Yellow encourages the growth of good energy and will rejuvenate a person's energy system.

White: White, although not technically a color, is used in similar situations as yellow to give energy. It boosts one's energy system by joining forces with the immune system to eliminate energy blockages.

Purple: Purple works somewhat the same as SEPs. It floats around until it finds blocked energy, then attaches to it like glue, penetrating the blockage and eliminating it from the inside out. Purple is one of if not *the* most difficult color to work with. Using purple takes tremendous focus and concentration, and if not properly applied, it will simply dissipate.

Red: Red is used as a healing color in the heat hologram. It is useful in the energetic treatment of cancer. Red can be used as a glue, which holds the areas to be healed in place. This enables me to then use the other healing colors to treat the area.

Blue: Blue is most effective in the form of positive thought. It is positive thought in liquid energy form. Blue prepares the body to be receptive to the healing intentionalities, thereby overshadowing any negative mind–body connections that may exist.

If each physical object emits its own hologram, how do you see multiple holograms for the same person?

When I connect to a person's hologram, all the holographic information contained within it becomes available to me. Each person emits just one hologram, but I am able to make better use of this information if I tune in to a specific view of it. Each holographic view, whether it's energetic, brain signals, real-time physical, or so on, constitutes a subset of all information contained within a person's hologram.

Think of this process as similar to your being an architect viewing blueprints of a proposed renovation. The existing building is physically in front of you, but the vision of the future or your goal or plan is what you must visualize in your mind's eye. Each future view can be seen on the blueprint. During a treatment, I redirect the energy flow of the holo-gram in accordance with the optimum state. At each stage between this perfect vision and the present health situation, adjustment and time are required. The problem must be removed, just as in a renova-tion. Most importantly, the person being treated and the healer must keep the vision of the desired end result in his mind's eyes. Some of the holographic images I see are more useful than others in viewing certain problems, just as some blueprints reveal cer-tain details more clearly than others. The electrical blueprint is needed for accessing certain informa-tion, while the floor plan is more useful for other aspects. All are needed in order to complete the ren-ovation.

Which colors do you use most often for healing?
I used to use purple most often, as it grabs hold of a problem most readily. This made removing energy blockages efficient. More often now I use

pure white energy, as this encompasses a much wider range of frequencies. Working with the full spectrum of light frequencies allows more healing energy to be absorbed by the person being treated. Everyone subconsciously knows where they need this healing energy, and white light is more diversified for people to use.

You often describe seeing problems in the body as green. Does this mean that the color green always indicates a problem?
Although I generally see problems in what I would describe as a fluorescent green, every person sees energy blockages and thus problems differently. It is all a matter of the healer's interpretation of the information he receives. Often the colors are beyond the physical spectrum, which makes what you are seeing difficult to describe in terms of color.

Chapter 6

Healing Histories

I don't need to be physically near someone to heal them.
Distance is not a factor.

—ADAM

is. Basically, I travel through the person's body and observe. This process I refer to as "seeing."

When I first started to heal, I was looking at only the most basic energy level. Now I am able to view many levels at once. I view several holograms of the person for energy diagnosis and healing. I am also able to bring up another person's hologram alongside to compare the different functions of the body. This is useful when I am not sure what a normal functioning body should look like. Now my healings are much more effective because I can approach the illness or injury from several fronts. I know there are many more levels for me to develop as I become more experienced.

Another important development of my gift is the ability to go down to the cellular level and actually see whether cells are in a precancerous or abnormal state that may lead to trouble. This is extremely important in energetically diagnosing illnesses before a dangerous situation develops.

I have enjoyed working with many people and find healing comes naturally for me. At first, it was important for me to work within a confidential and isolated group in order to develop and understand my gift. My school life and personal friends had to be kept separate from my healing work. For this reason, I saw people whom my parents knew weren't associated with my friends. Most came as nonbelievers and skeptics and left in awe.

As my skills developed and people began hearing about me by word of mouth, I started to be contacted by others in the healing profession. I worked with a group of naturopathic doctors who consulted me when the patient was interested in my ability. One such patient was an elderly lady with an extremely sore leg. I immediately pointed to an area on her hip as the source of the pain. It was nowhere near where she felt the pain. When the doctor touched the spot on her hip, an area where two muscle groups met, the woman's leg flew up, nearly kicking him. "That's it!" she exclaimed. "That's where the problem is!"

Working with these doctors was a great experience for me. I was given no background information about the patients beforehand, yet every diagnosis I gave was accurate.

MY MOST DIFFICULT HEALING

Last year, my parents decided to take the family to Mexico for a break from the healings and all the emails we were constantly receiving. I felt that I needed a brain break, and I knew that a rest would make me more powerful. We also thought that it would be exciting to spend Christmas in a different country.

The vacation got off to a great start. We stayed in a resort, part of an all-inclusive package, where my sister and I could order drinks all day. My dad made sure the bartender knew how old we were. As soon as we arrived, he took my sister and me to meet the bartender. He introduced us as his son and daughter and informed him that "they don't drink alcohol." We were able to order endless virgin strawberry daiquiris, though.

Two days into our vacation, my dad was playing with my sister and me in the resort's swimming pool. Dad had just thrown my sister into the air and over his head. At the same time, I was surfacing out of the water just behind him. The timing couldn't have been worse. My sister landed on my head, fracturing one of my neck vertebrae. Numbness spread down my body. It was a cold feeling. I somehow managed to get out of the water before I lost feeling in my legs.

My parents called an ambulance. The pain in my neck was unlike anything I had ever experienced. I felt like I should pass out, but I knew I was the only one who could fix my neck. Despite my pain, I was able to go in and see it. It was bad.

It was very difficult to heal myself because I was in excruciating pain. When I try to view an injury in my own body, it always looks foggy. I had to try my hardest to use all the power at my disposal. I worked on the fracture and the swelling for about half an hour. In that time, I could see that I had managed to heal the fracture and bring the swelling down. It is important to reduce the swelling as quickly as possible, because the swelling itself can create problems. By the time the ambulance arrived, I was walking, but the attendants insisted I put on a neck brace and go to the hospital.

X-rays were done on my neck as soon as I arrived at the hospital. The neurologist arrived with his little reflex hammer. He checked to see that all my reflexes were working. I passed with flying colors. When the doctors looked at the X-rays, they pointed out that I had a congenital defect on my C2 vertebra. Otherwise, everything was fine.

I knew that the defect was not congenital. It was the area that I had just damaged and subsequently healed. My parents brought the X-rays home so that we could compare them with ones taken a few years ago when I injured my shoulder playing tennis. As I expected, there was no sign of a defect on the earlier X-rays.

I felt that I had passed a major test of willpower and healing ability. I surprised even myself with what one can do if confronted with the need. It had been more difficult than any other healing I had done.

CHRONIC ILLNESS

Living with chronic illness is a reality for millions of people—children as well as adults. Out of necessity, people get used to tolerating constant pain, so this to them becomes the normal state of health. Many have forgotten the pain-free time of their lives. In order to heal, they must first remember this. They must have a contrast in their mind and set their goals accordingly.

A number of people with chronic illness have come to me. Because the illness has been with them for so many years, many think that it might take a lot of work to fix. Sometimes it does, but not always.

Under the Western medical system, there are no cures for many illnesses—just ways to manage and live with them. Sadly, this has caused some people to give up hope of ever getting better. However, I have treated a number of these people, and their pain is sometimes eliminated within two or three treatments. Often one treatment produces amazing results. These results have been long lasting and in many cases the chronic problem has been eliminated.

One man came to me with a sore neck that had been bothering him for four years. I quickly found the problem and spent about five minutes treating him. He reported that he felt immediate relief. He was amazed that for the first time in four years his neck was not sore or stiff. I guess he felt so good that he decided to go skiing. Unfortunately, he re-injured his neck and I had to do another treatment. The second treatment was also successful, but this time I made sure he understood that muscles and ligaments take a bit of time to adjust to the new state of wellness. I asked him to refrain from any physical strain for a while.

The return to health is a process, meaning a sequence of changes must occur. The mind is already there or the healing wouldn't have occurred. The mind and the body are connected, but the mind can get there quicker than the physical body can. People I have treated must gradually let their bodies catch up. It takes time. Those who have suffered with chronic pain for years frequently overexert themselves at first, since they feel so good and are so glad to be pain-free. In their enthusiasm, they sometimes return to activities they have been unable to do for a long time, before the body has had a chance to finish the healing process. It is important to give the body sufficient time to complete the process.

Another fellow came to me with a sore back that had been bothering him for years. When I went in, I could see that the third and fifth disks in his lower back were damaged. He confirmed that these areas had been diagnosed as the problem but didn't think anything could be done about it. I treated him, and his back pain has improved considerably. He returns from time to time for maintenance treatments. It is very rewarding for me to be able to help people who have suffered for years.

I had the pleasure of meeting a woman who was planning her wedding yet was in too much pain to try on shoes for her big day. She was motivated to improve her health, so we began treatments. As a preteen, she was athletically inclined. Competitive sports kept her schedule full. With a mix of summer and winter activities, she was always on the go. Then she started feeling extreme pain in her arms and legs. A diagnosis of fibromyalgia soon followed. As many people with chronic pain experience, the sleepless nights became a major problem in and of themselves. Fatigue rules the day and night. Next, depression set in, as she was unable to continue with her activities. She had to change her active pastimes to sedentary ones in an attempt to adapt to her limitations.

This act of redefining self is difficult. One grieves for one's old self and past abilities. We all redefine ourselves gradually throughout our lifetimes. Illness or injury often forces this upon one without any adjustment period. Feeling like an eighty-year-old is expected if you are eighty. However, if you are a teenager, or even twenty or thirty for that matter, the physical pain is accompanied with feelings of resentment. How could this happen? Why did this happen to me? This is so unfair!

I started doing energy treatments with the bride-to-be and felt positive about it. She felt tingling throughout her body and got goose pimples. They were powerful experiences for her; she could feel a storm of energy moving inside her. Sometimes she became dizzy and pale right after the treatment. The day following a treatment, she always reported that she slept well right through the night, which was unusual for her. Upon waking, she felt refreshed. After four treatments, she felt reenergized. It certainly helped that she was sleeping right through the night. She had a wonderful time on her wedding day, too!

I treated a man who had chronic pain after being involved in a bad car accident many years ago. He had little success with conventional medicine and requested my help. Immediately after the first treatment he noticed that his constant headache had vanished. He also had digestive problems, particularly stomach aches, caused by injuries he had sustained in the accident. These too disappeared. As is often the case, physical recovery led to significant improvement in his ability to focus and concentrate on mental tasks.

A woman contacted me who had had severe chronic asthma for many years. When I looked at her photograph I could see a haze over her lungs and the airways leading to them. With most lung conditions, I apply heat to the hologram, as I find that this is the most efficient way to correct it. During the treatment she felt the heat that I applied, followed by a tingling sensation. Instantly she felt that her lungs were lighter and more elastic. Breathing was easier for her and she became so relaxed that she fell asleep. As a result of unlabored breathing, her mind was clearer.

I was also contacted by a woman in her fifties who had peripheral neuropathy, which caused painful nerve sensations. Shortly after the treatment began, she noticed that the constant sensations of numbness, pins and needles, and burning in her extremities had left her. She felt that her quality of life had returned.

A woman who had chronic stomach problems called me. She told me that she ate poorly and felt tired most of the time. In addition, she said she rarely slept and suffered from occasional depression. The morning following her first distant treatment, she woke up pain-free. Her stomach did not ache with every breath she took as it had before. Her new painless state brought with it a feeling of peace.

A man who had been in a bad accident many years ago contacted me requesting a treatment. He is quadriplegic and since he was diagnosed with a complete spinal sever, I cautioned him to have no expectations going into the treatment but to keep an open mind. During the treatment he noticed that his triceps and biceps were tingling, whereas he had had no feeling in them for the last twenty years. He also had experienced chronic pain and stiffness in his neck and shoulders, which reduced in intensity after the treatment. He was most excited about the tingling that he felt in his lower body.

I met a woman who had been diagnosed with syringomyelia, a degenerative spinal condition. After one treatment her pain was significantly reduced, allowing her to stand erect and to roll over comfortably while sleeping. Now she was able to sleep through the night, making all the difference to her outlook.

INJURIES

I have had the opportunity to work with several athletes who had sports-related injuries. One baseball player had thrown out his shoulder by pitching. He hadn't been able to play any sports after that and was in constant pain. The movement of his shoulder was restricted. After one treatment, he was pain-free and he regained his full range of motion in his shoulder. Many sports injuries are fairly quickly resolved with treatments.

CANCER

One of the things that I find interesting is how the inside of a person's body looks when she is undergoing or has undergone chemotherapy. It looks like a war zone. Cells are fighting each other in an exhaustive battle of survival, and it doesn't look like there are any real victors.

I am often amazed by how fast the cancer or a tumor can grow. If I go in to a person whose cancer has advanced throughout her entire system, it is almost impossible for me to stay ahead of the growth. I am much more optimistic about influencing cancer when it has not spread. It is more straightforward to focus on an isolated area, such as an organ.

Standard Western therapies to destroy tumor cells include radiation and chemical treatments. The genetic code tells cells to grow and divide, thus spreading the cancer. Radiation is energy and it is used in cancer therapy to destroy the cancer cells or alter cell activity and slow growth. But radiation also affects normal cells, which in turn causes side effects, such as nausea. Many radiation treatments will prolong a person's life. Chemotherapy may also be recommended, causing even more side effects in a body that is already ravaged. In making decisions about cancer treatment, the quality of life should be an issue. It is a delicate balance. Of course, sometimes chemotherapy and radiation is successful.

On an energetic level, I see the cells within a living organism communicate with one another. Cancer cells are no exception. I also see on the energetic level that cancer cells absorb energy and modify according to intention. When cancer cells communicate, they pass on information about any changes within their immediate environment. When I am energetically treating cancer, the death of the cancer has a domino effect. One cancer cell appears to receive the energy, modifies itself according to intention and passes the message along to the next cell. The surrounding healthy cells are not damaged because they are not modified. The only side effects are slight, and are from the body adjusting to being healthy again.

This technique is applicable only to cancer that is localized, such as a single tumor, not to a malignant spread. Imagine a sealed-in city occupied by cancer cells with no communication with the outside world. The only communication is with one another. When I make energetic changes to the cancer cells, they spread the news around to each other, and in this way cause their own destruction.

If the cancer is spread out, as it is with advanced lung cancers, there are cancer cells outside the "city" that could warn the rest of the cancer and prevent the changes required to kill them off. In effect, I "see" that the cancer cells at the first cancer site send distress signals to the other cancer locations. In this situation, I resort to a combination of reasonably high intensity yellow, purple and white light energy. I would not use light that is focused like a laser because the cancer is spread out too much for that to be effective.

Sometimes during treatment the person can feel the activity or process. Some people describe it as a tingling sensation in the area I am treating. Others feel as though ping-pong balls are ricocheting inside them. Occasionally, people feel sleepy (some have even fallen fast asleep during the treatment) or dizzy or nauseous. And some people feel nothing. Everyone is different. How they feel it, or even if they feel it, doesn't seem to affect the outcome of my treatment.

HEALING RONNIE HAWKINS

On September 21, 2002, I read an article in our local paper on rock legend Ronnie Hawkins. It reported that he had been diagnosed with inoperable pancreatic cancer. I had never heard of Ronnie Hawkins before, but my dad told me he enjoys his music.

Ronnie Hawkins has lived in Ontario since the late 1950s, when he immigrated to Canada from his native Arkansas. Many consider Ronnie to have been the performer who brought rock and roll to Canada. Ronnie is perhaps best known outside of Canada for his backing band—some major stars played in it at one time or another. The original name of The Band, legendary in the 1960s for backing Bob Dylan, was The Hawks. Ronnie has been in the business for decades. When John Lennon and Yoko Ono were in town during their 1969 peace crusade, they stayed at Ronnie's place.

I had not healed anyone of pancreatic cancer before but I wanted to try to help Ronnie. According to the newspaper article, on August 13, 2002, Ronnie had surgery to remove the tumor. However, when the doctor cut him open, he saw that the tumor was much larger than the anticipated three centimeters. It was wrapped around an artery and couldn't be removed. Chemotherapy was apparently not an option for Ronnie. His cancer was diagnosed as terminal, and I thought he might be interested in my healing ability.

I contacted Ronnie's daughter-in-law, who is his manager. Mary was open-minded and felt that they had nothing to lose by seeing me. Talking to Mary, I realized that Ronnie wasn't just a rock legend but a loving husband, father of three and grandfather. There were a lot of worried relatives.

When I had looked at Ronnie's photo, my first impression was that he was an honest man. When I told Mary this, she said that comment shook her. Ronnie is as honest as they come, she said, and one of the funniest people you will ever meet. Ronnie was quite willing to try my healing approach, since the doctors had not held out much hope for him. Distant healing was certainly a new idea to Ronnie and his family, but they were keen. "If Adam can pull this off, tell him we'll send him an autographed Hawk T-shirt," Ronnie said with his trademark good humor. "Five of the best doctors in the world have told me that this is it. They said three to six months, tops—I'm gone."

In September 2002, well-known Canadian producer and composer David Foster, also an alumnus of Ronnie's backing band, hosted an intimate gathering in Ronnie's honor in Toronto. Many major celebrities attended, including former U.S. president Bill Clinton, comedian Whoopi Goldberg, singer and composer Paul Anka, Ronnie's tycoon friend Don Tyson from Arkansas and Canadian industrialist Peter Pocklington. Paul Anka had written another version of his song "My Way" and dedicated it to Ronnie. Bill Clinton, David Foster and Paul Anka sang their parts of the song. Ronnie, with his wife, Wanda, at his side, had his guests laughing through their tears throughout the evening.

A few weeks later, the City of Toronto declared October 4 Ronnie Hawkins Day. That day started off with Ronnie being inducted into Canada's Walk of Fame. Many people feel that it was an induction long overdue. Usually, this recognition is formally made in May of each year. However, because of the dire state of Ronnie's health, it was done a few months early, in October.

That evening a tribute concert was held at Massey Hall to honor Ronnie. Ronnie got up on stage and joined his band with the song "Hey Bo Diddley." Kris Kristofferson and the Tragically Hip highlighted a special four-hour concert of stars. "If there is a God of rock 'n' roll, I know he looks just like this guy," Kris Kristofferson said in his tribute.

When I first went into Ronnie's hologram on September 21, 2002, I could see a tumor the size of a tennis ball—approximately ten centimeters in diameter. I spent the next few weeks treating Ronnie's tumor on the energetic level, helping his body fight off the cancer and reduce the tumor. From the beginning of my treatment, Ronnie felt a quivering in his abdomen. His jaundice improved and his overall health seemed to be getting better. He no longer felt or looked like a dying man. On September 23, 2002, I got news that he was looking wonderful. Everyone was encouraged, especially Ronnie. He told me to "Keep on rockin."

I continued treating Ronnie intensely every day. We all felt positive about the treatments. On September 27, 2002, I energetically compared Ronnie's pancreatic functioning to that of my dad's. I did this by visually bringing in front of me the quantum hologram screens of both. I noticed that Ronnie's pancreas was blocked and my dad's had a constant drip. I manipulated the energy and got Ronnie's pancreatic juices flowing. From what I saw energetically, it started with a gushing flow; there was probably a lot of buildup. My parents spent a sleepless night worrying about this, but I assured them that his body knew how to regulate it. I later learned that the pancreas secretes insulin and many enzymes which would have been blocked by the tumor.

Ronnie continued to feel and look great, and his blood sugar levels improved. He was walking better and his eyes looked clearer. Ronnie *wanted* to get better. He has such a love for life. This is his greatest strength.

By the time November arrived, rather than planning a funeral, Ronnie was planning a CD release and a TV show. Ronnie continued to feel better and the fluttering feeling in his abdomen persisted. I could see energetically that the cancer was gone and that the remaining tumor tissue, no longer growing, was being removed by Ronnie's own system. This takes time, which explains why the quivering in his abdomen continued. But he was now thinking more about living than dying.

A CT scan done on November 14, 2002, determined that Ronnie's tumor was approximately four and a half centimeters. From its original ten centimeter mass I had seen on the energetic level, the tumor had shrunk in half. But the doctors still believed that Ronnie had cancer and was going to die.

On November 27, 2002, Ronnie had a biopsy to check on the cancer. The biopsy was negative. There was no cancer.

All the treatments I did on Ronnie were from three thousand miles away. I started working on Ronnie's energy system September 21, 2002, a month and a half after the surgeon sewed him back up and told him there wasn't anything he could do for him. The doctor expected that Ronnie would not live to see Christmas. I treated his energy system on a daily basis for a few weeks and fairly regularly after that. All my indications on the energy level were that his body had managed to kill the cancer and that the tumor was shrinking rapidly.

On February 27, 2003, Ronnie's CT scan showed no evidence of any tumor. He now performs onstage with his band and sings all night. This is an amazing change because it was only months before that he was a dying man. An MRI done April 11, 2003, confirmed that Ronnie is cancer-free.

Shortly afterward, my autographed T-shirt arrived safely in the mail. I have since met Ronnie and his family on several occasions and we enjoy keeping in touch.

Why was healing yourself the most difficult healing?
Generally, when I am treating myself it is similar to treating anyone else, so it is quite straightforward for me to do. However, when my spine was fractured I was in excruciating pain, which made it difficult to concentrate. It took a great deal of concentration just to stay conscious. This is why healing myself in this instance was so challenging.

Why is it that it can take months from the time you start treatments until you get positive confirmation through scans and tests?
Many variables are involved in any treatment. People's thoughts, emotions, beliefs and attitudes differ, as well as their lifestyle habits. The illness may be categorized similarly, but how it develops and manifests itself may vary considerably.

Generally, a person with a more positive outlook

notices beneficial effects sooner than someone with a less positive attitude. An illness that has just recently developed reacts more quickly to treatments than does a chronic condition that has existed for many years.

The first treatment I did on Ronnie Hawkins for his terminal pancreatic cancer was on September 21, 2002, and seven months later his MRI scan showed no evidence of a tumor. During this time I did about sixty treatments from a distance of about three thousand miles. I sometimes worked intensely for forty minutes in one session. Energy treatments are not a magic wand, and their efficacy has as much to do with the person being treated as with the healer.

Chapter 7
The Learning Continues

What is in the mind is always reflected in the body.

—ADAM

to me after treating many people with similar problems. However, I've discovered that people react differently to each type of treatment, whether it's one of conventional medicine or energy healing.

Each person's journey to wellness is an individual process. Healing the *person* rather than just eliminating the ailment is vital. Sometimes the cause of disease is a poor lifestyle choice, such as improper diet, lack of exercise, smoking, drinking or taking excessive drugs (be they street drugs or prescription drugs). I've had to set some tough boundaries for those people who continue to make choices that will negatively affect their health. For example, when a person with a smoking-related disease continues to smoke, treating him or her would not result in recovery, as the root of the problem has not been addressed. In one man I was treating, I could see abnormal cells continue to develop. I knew that if he continued to smoke cigarettes, there would be no point in giving him healing energy, as the cancer would generate faster than I could kill it. I informed him that he *had* to quit smoking, and he did when I told him that I would not attempt further treatments until he did. Often lifestyle changes *must* be made in order for the person to be healed.

It is also difficult for me to see clearly inside bodies of people who are on medication. Ideally, I do the treatment just before it is time for a person to take the medication. This usually allows me to see clearly enough to carry out a treatment. I saw a forty-year-old woman who had been in a debilitating car accident and was on painkillers and anti-inflammatory drugs. The medications made the energy blockages jelly-like and I was unable to move them during treatments. I suggested that she reschedule another treatment that would be just *before* she took her medication. When she did, I found her energy blockages much easier to move, and she reported that she noticed the positive effects more intensely.

Muscular and structural maladies are fairly straightforward. They are easy for me to spot on the body, as I see breaks in the person's aura. I can go in and show the body its natural energy grid. Sometimes the injury or whatever is causing the malady is so old that the body has forgotten what the natural healthy state is like. It is very helpful if I can show it the map of health. The body is an amazing thing and will strive to return to a healthy state if given the chance. Reminding the body of this ideal state and providing a push in the right direction is sometimes all that is needed.

Another thing I have learned is that some people have underlying psychological and emotional issues that affect the energy body and so must be addressed before healing can take place. A person's negativity, guilt or fear will work against the path to wellness. Be prepared for some personal work and perhaps some lifestyle changes if you want to achieve a lasting state of wellness.

I remember going in to help one woman and thinking that I couldn't do anything for her. The antidepressants she had just taken prevented me from doing my healing. So we rescheduled the healing to a time of day when she hadn't just taken her medication. During that treatment, I was able to remove some energy blockages, but I intuitively noted a strong psychological basis to the illness. This became obvious, as the problems immediately rebounded after treatment, which is common for emotionally based illnesses unless the root cause is dealt with. She mentioned that, before I treated her, there were about five other unrelated problems bothering her. My feeling was that she needed to address the underlying origin of these concerns before I could improve her state of wellness.

One man I treated had a stomach condition with symptoms similar to those experienced by people with irritable bowel syndrome. Those symptoms include abdominal pains, severe diarrhea and reactions to certain foods. He claimed to be allergic to milk or dairy products and took great pains to avoid these foods. I went in and took a look. I could see that his stomach was irritated, but I could see no physical cause. I am not saying that it was all in his head. I know that the symptoms he experienced were real to him—and painful. It seemed to me that he processed his emotions and his anxieties through his stomach. I suspect that if he hadn't created the stomach condition, he might have had to create another physical malady. I could treat this man every day, but his condition would return by the mind. For the body to return to a state of total health, these issues of attention and recognition must be addressed. One can't just heal the body and expect lasting effects if the mind is not in alignment with this objective.

Avoidance behavior is another root cause of disease. For instance, a person may be suffering from a work-related injury because that person is desiring a new career. But switching careers can be a scary thing, even if the person wants it: A major life change is not an easy thing for many people to make. Creating the chronic condition replaces the desired change.

Family members can also be a factor in our health, by affecting the decisions we make about our health and treatment. One day, I received an email from a woman who was clearly panicked. She had terminal cancer. She did not want to pursue chemotherapy or radiation, but wanted to explore energy healing. Her family wanted her to have chemotherapy and radiation. Even after X-rays showed that the tumors had significantly shrunk after several of my treatments, she continued to waffle about chemotherapy because of the pressure from relatives. Eventually she decided to go the route of chemotherapy.

For the most part, however, people are ready, willing and accepting of my energy treatments. With that receptivity and a positive attitude, I have had the honor and pleasure of helping many people return to health. For some, however, it is their time. A man whose elderly father was in an extended-care hospital after suffering a stroke contacted me. He was concerned that his father was dying. I went to the hospital to do an in-person treatment on the father. He was lying in bed and was nonresponsive when I first saw him. During the treatment, I saw a strong spirit in the man, and I could tell that it was not his time yet to die, but that it was near. The next day, after only one treatment, he was able to sit up in bed, talk and even complain about the food. A couple of months later, his entire family came from out of the country to visit him. By this time, he was well enough to leave the hospital on a day pass and go with all of them to his favorite restaurant, and he even purchased a lottery ticket. He died later during their visit, but he died peacefully, having been able to say his goodbyes to those he loved.

Another thing I have learned from my healings is that many people are interested in energy healing only as a last resort, rather than as a first choice. This doesn't make sense to me, as I personally would be most interested in trying the least invasive treatment first. I have been contacted by several people with cancer who have been through surgery, chemotherapy and radiation. Now that they are terminal, they ask for my help. The majority of cells in their bodies are either cancerous or negatively affected by the disease or the medical treatments they have undergone. Energy healing is often considered only as a last resort, after every other avenue has been exhausted.

I had a father email me a week before Christmas with an urgent plea. His son had leukemia, and had a fever of 105 degrees Fahrenheit and blood in his urine. He and his wife were staying in a motel near the hospital where his son had been a patient for many months. He had no idea how he was going to pay the $100,000 hospital bill, a bill that was climbing each day. All he and his wife knew was that they desperately wanted their son to get better.

When I looked at the boy, I knew right away that his body had decided to shut down. All I could do was give him positive encouragement and some energy. I managed to get his temperature down below a hundred degrees for a couple of days. He was actually able to get out of bed and play with his toys—something he had not done for weeks. However, the illness was too far along to halt and he died on Christmas Eve.

I never realized how many sick people there are in the world until I was able to do something about it. Most of the people I see are in need of some positive thoughts as part of their healing. By the time they have turned to something they view as radical, such as energy healing, they have usually already been turned away by the mainstream Western medical system. Being told that there is nothing more that can be done and that you will die in six months' time is not easy to hear.

But sometimes it is a self-fulfilling prophecy to be told that you will die in six months. (Of course, often patients themselves demand to know.) Keep in mind that the brain is like a supercomputer that interprets incoming information. Any thoughts are greatly influenced by what we experience. In addition to our own thoughts, our brain is constantly being fed information by those around us and will respond to positive or negative thoughts accordingly. We must take control of this computer rather than allowing it to control us. What I am suggesting is that no one rush quickly to a conclusion when there might indeed be something that can still be done. Exhaust *all* possibilities.

We must always keep in mind that everything in the human body is interconnected, and one change, whether a dysfunction or improvement, affects everything else. This is very important for people to realize, both in a personal and a global context. According to this perspective of interconnectedness, we are at one with the whole existence of all time and space, all interwoven into a unified state of being.

What do you "see" as an illness signature; for example, how would you describe the multiple sclerosis signature that you see?

The first time I looked at someone with MS was when I helped my mom with her trigeminal neural-gia. I saw this painful symptom as a throbbing fluorescent green ball of light in her head and instinctively pulled it out of her. At the time, I didn't reflect much on the signature of the illness, as I had no reference point. Since then, I recognize MS as fluorescent green flecks of sand that appear to be bubbling up through the spinal cord and into the brain. I tried removing them from my mom's holo-gram, but it was like trying to separate different colors of sand with my fingers. It wasn't effective at all. Then I used my imagination and decided to visualize vacuuming up the sand particles. This was far more useful. While using visualizations, if one way presents a difficulty, I find another approach. I need to be creative and flexible.

Does the medication a person is taking cloud your vision when you go in? What do you actually see?

What I see depends on the person involved and the particular drug they are taking. Even off-the-shelf and over-the-counter medications can affect how clearly I see. Of course, the more toxic the drug, the more obscured everything appears. When someone is on strong medications, it often seems as though I am viewing his reflection in a warped mirror. Other times the reflection appears cloudy, misty or foggy.

Sometimes the medication gives a blockage a jelly-like texture that is difficult to grip on to when I attempt to remove it. However, bombarding the blockage with energy helps a great deal because the body knows what the problem is and will direct the energy appropriately. The person receiving the energy bursts intuitively knows where to focus his attention. If I'm unable to move the energy block, I suggest rescheduling the treatment to a time when the medication is not so intensely present in the person's body—usually shortly before he is due to take the medication.

Does a person have to believe in energy treatments for them to work?

It certainly helps. We all have many filters through which we sift incoming information. These filters are our beliefs. We can have so many of them that virtually nothing gets past them. When this happens, we are our own worst enemies, as we have effectively blinded ourselves to all possibilities.

When one is blind to the potential of energy treatments, nothing can get through. An open mind will allow change as long as one can be flexible to incoming information. Of course, if you truly believe that energy is the invisible power of you and the universe, your possibilities are limitless. As with everything else in life, you are responsible for your own limitations.

Chapter 8
The Return to Health Is a Process

You must step out of the box of conventional thinking.
You need courage to take that step.

—ADAM

Disease is the absence of health. It is an energy system out of balance. It is a body that is not recognizing its natural grid, or code, for proper functioning. Disease can take many forms. Sometimes it shows itself as chronic pain. Sometimes the body will grow a tumor. Sometimes it will grow cancer. There are many ways that disease can manifest itself, and there are just as many causes for it.

Ideal health is a state of no energy blockages, where energy flows freely throughout the body. Everything works together in harmony. There is no physical, energetic or emotional conflict in the body. Perfect balance exists.

Perfect health should be everybody's goal. Old scars and injuries make achieving it impossible, but we can work toward achieving the best balance possible within these limitations.

ATTITUDE IS IMPORTANT

From beginning to end, attitude is important. Whatever a person's religious or spiritual beliefs are, they should be maintained during treatment, as they are important to that person and therefore to the healing process. No matter what one's belief system is, the most important factor of all is a positive attitude. *Believe* that good things are going to happen.

Attitude is a powerful tool in the healing process and is the foundation for returning one's body to good health. A person must be able to show thanks to others and be thankful for the good things in her life. By dwelling on the bad things in our lives, we are unable to appreciate all the good.

You must step out of the box of conventional thinking. You need courage to take that step. There is no authority other than you as to whether healing (or anything else, for that matter) is going to work. People delegate authority to others who are deemed as experts. Perhaps they feel that it relieves them of the responsibility, but it doesn't. The choice and authority is still ultimately yours. Courage and a positive attitude will lead you along your path to wellness.

Each of us can achieve our own personal best with a positive attitude. Having an open mind will help you achieve any goal. And I believe that all people have a certain degree of power to heal themselves and others. It is merely that some people are more sensitive to the universal energy connection, just as some of us have a natural gift for playing the piano or playing sports. The point is that we may not all be Mozart or Tiger Woods, but we can all learn to play the piano or golf if we dedicate the time and our focus. I think it's the same for what I do. We can all do it if we try hard enough.

WORRY IS A WASTE

Worry is a waste of time. Worry is fear of the future, which has yet to be determined. It is harmful. It is harmful to the worrier and to everyone close to that person. Nothing good comes of worry.

Worry leads to guilt. Guilt leads to negativity and loss of self-empowerment, and then it affects our health. And then it affects everyone around us through our interconnectedness. Some people are so disconnected from themselves and their own energy systems that relating to others and the connectedness is challenging.

Worry can cause disease. I can make the body aware that things can be different, but unless the person I'm doing the treatment on can see through his own negativity, nothing will change. This will affect the efficacy of the treatments. It is far easier for me to treat someone with terminal cancer and a positive attitude than someone who has a minor ailment but a negative attitude.

Some people cannot get out of their negative thought loop. If you say, "Hey, isn't it a wonderful sunny day?" they reply with something like, "Yeah, but it's probably going to rain tomorrow." They are insulated by negativity. From past experiences, they paste various negative labels on life. The excuses range from parents to guilt issues. They tend to blame others, especially their parents, but that is useless. Whatever your excuse is, you've got to deal with these issues and move on.

VISUALIZATION

Never underestimate the power of visualization. When you are imagining, you are visualizing. When you are visualizing, you are accessing the universal knowledge base, scientifically known as the field of quantum information. Intuition is the ability to tap into this field that surrounds all of us and emanates throughout the universe.

See yourself in the state of wellness you want to achieve. Do this in as much detail as you can. *See* yourself doing what you will do in this state of wellness. *Feel* how it will feel in this state. *Hear* the sounds you will hear around you. *Smell* the air. Do this every day. Make time for it, and look forward to spending this time with yourself each day. This state of wellness is your personal goal, your dream. Your dream of your path to wellness will help you achieve your goal.

Therapists have helped people by suggestion. They ask their patients to visualize the illness in their body and then have them visualize its removal by various means. When doing this, the mind is telling the body to heal itself. This might be successful with a few people who have a vivid imagination and are able to hold the healing thoughts for long periods. What I do is similar except that I influence the mind–body controls and bypass the person's need to successfully carry out the task of visualization. If someone was able to do this visualization while I do my healing, that would make my job easier.

INTUITIVENESS

As with any modality of healing, the beliefs and goals of the healer are as important as those of the person being healed. In this and the following sections, I elaborate on my own beliefs based on what I have experienced so far. Whether you agree with the specific details is not what is important, but understanding the beliefs I bring to energy healing will help increase your comfort level, and this in turn will help in your healing process and, thus, your return to health.

My ability to tap into the knowledge base that surrounds us is always improving. When I first started healing, I had to see a picture of someone in order to receive any information on them. Now, when someone simply mentions a name, I sometimes make the connection to that person. When I tap into information on a person this way, it goes through the person mentioning the name, so if someone else has the same name, I still connect to the right person. The path of linking to another person happens very fast, and I have not been able to map it out or even fully understand it yet.

Intuitiveness can be a strange thing. My parents were going to a friend's house for dinner one night and they told me who was going to be there. The name of one person brought an image into my mind of his ex-wife. They had been separated for ten years. I mentioned that she had some kind of neurological problem that was affecting her reasoning. I also said that this happened about ten years ago and that she was doing much better now. At the dinner, my parents were able to confirm that all of this had taken place.

I usually know or sense what is wrong with a person before she says anything or before I go in and see. Of course, I get much more detail when I actually go in and look at the person's energy system. When I am healing someone, I receive intuitive information as well as visual holograms. I feel that this is because of the interconnectedness of everyone. Again, the television provides a good analogy of the way I can receive the information. With the remote control, you can change the channels and connect to different movies. When I go into a person, I don't have to manually change the channels; they are changed instantaneously by thought. I believe that the information I access is coming from the field of quantum information.

To continue the television analogy, suppose that you want to watch a particular movie. Now imagine that your remote control can read your thoughts. The device picks up your thought and switches the television channel to the station showing the movie. This is similar to what happens when I scan a person for injury or disease.

The controls that I use are extremely sophisticated. I might tune in to the person's doctor's information, or in to the person's mother because of their close association or in to someone who might be aware of this person's injury. All the information I obtain is pertinent to the injury and becomes part of my analysis. In this way I am connecting to the field of quantum information for my healing.

This intuitive ability to receive images goes hand in hand with the healing. I see what and where the problem is, and I collect the intuitive information to complete my healing treatment. The information I receive is not in words but in images. They must be interpreted into something I can explain. Much of the time I use my own nonmedical terms to describe what I can see in a person.

I looked at a woman who had a total hysterectomy. She had endometriosis—the endometrial tissue, which lines the uterus, had attached to other organs in the pelvic cavity. She had the hysterectomy ten years ago, and although her uterus was removed, some of the endometrial tissue still remained on the other organs. The doctors said they could do nothing about it. The tissue I saw had connected to the kidneys. It looked like a plant growing on the outside of the kidneys, which at the time seemed strange to me. But after she described her health history, it all made sense.

Another woman had a problem with fluid in her lungs. She said that she could feel the fluid but was unable to cough it up. I went in and looked at her lungs. I told her that the inside of her lungs looked like they were sealed with some kind of coating. The liquid that she felt in her lungs was behind this coating. She then informed me that she had an operation for breast cancer and the doctors had to apply a sealant on the inside of her lungs after that operation. This explained what I saw in her lungs.

The image information I receive is not always exactly as it appears physically, which can be a challenge for me. One man I looked at had damaged disks in his lower back. What I saw was his lower spine being held in place by two thin perpendicular strings. My interpretation of this was instability in the lower back. He confirmed that his doctor had told him exactly that only a few days before my seeing him.

Intuitive abilities are becoming a major part of my energetic healing and diagnosis. Now, at the mere mention of someone's name, I am sometimes able to pick up information that lets me know what the problem is and whether I am able to help. And sometimes I receive information that isn't directly relevant to the injury. For example, I gave a woman one treatment and then didn't hear from her again. I knew it had helped her, but I also knew that her husband was against this type of treatment and was trying to talk her out of it. She eventually did contact me, and when I mentioned this issue to her, she wanted to know how I knew. Her husband had indeed tried to talk her out of it, but she had decided to proceed because her arthritis had improved so much after just one treatment with me. Since then, her arthritis has improved considerably.

When I look at a person, I can often tell whether or not he will be receptive to energy healing. I can also frequently see if it is a person's time to die. There isn't much that I can do if this is the case. When the body decides that it can't hang on anymore, it shows signs of shutting down. This is evident to me, and I feel that it would be futile to try to reverse it. I can give that person energy and in some cases help him become more accepting of the inevitable.

I feel that I am constantly in touch with the field of quantum information. It doesn't take much thinking for me to quickly connect to a certain area of the hologram. I also believe that this will get stronger as I grow older and more experienced.

INSIGHTS

Being able to tap into the field of quantum information opens my consciousness up to receive information about many things. The information available is vast. Sometimes I receive knowledge about events that will occur in the near or distant future. I believe the mind does some sort of instantaneous statistical analysis of all the information available and comes up with a probable event. This is similar to the ability that Edgar Cayce had to make some incredible predictions.

Edgar Cayce (1877–1945) was one of the most amazing psychics ever. He was able to diagnose illness in people he had never met, and then prescribe the medical treatment to heal them. He was also a devout Christian who wrote volumes of studies on how clairvoyance and reincarnation are not in contradiction to the teachings of the Bible. I recommend the reading of his material to anyone with an interest in this. Edgar Cayce became renowned for his ability to make predictions about future events. Many (but not all) of his predictions turned out to be correct.

If everything were to happen exactly as he foresaw from that moment, the prediction would come true. If a prediction did not come true it was probably because what he predicted was in a snapshot of time, but an unforeseen event came into the picture. Let's take a horse race as an analogy. A person reads the statistics on a horse and it seems there is no way it can lose the race. All the other horses are real duds and the horse you want to bet on once won the Kentucky Derby. The track is dry and this is when your horse does its best. For an instant in time, everything points to your horse easily winning the race. As the race gets under way, your horse gets bumped by another horse, causing it to break an ankle. So much for that prediction. Unforeseen events altered what seemed like a predictable outcome.

It is the same with psychic predictions except more information is involved. The closer the prediction is to the event, the more likely it is to happen. I was driving home one night with my dad. It was around ten o'clock. All of a sudden I told my dad, "I feel death coming." I said it was a horrible feeling and that hundreds of people were going to die soon. He told me not to worry and that we could check the newspapers in the morning. But my dad's driving became more cautious, as though he was beginning to wonder if we were about to be involved in an accident.

The next morning when we read the newspaper, we learned that an airplane had left Taipei, Taiwan, at 3 P.M. and went off the radar screen about twenty minutes after takeoff. Over two hundred people died in the crash. We checked the time difference and the time that it went off the radar was exactly when I had the feeling of death coming. Why did I get this feeling? Perhaps I got an energy connection from one of the people on board the plane. Or perhaps it was because so many people were heading for death at once, and because they knew it, I was able to pick up on their emotional distress.

REINCARNATION

Whether reincarnation is part of your belief system or not will not affect your healing process. This is just another level of spirituality that I personally accept. In the cycle of life, death is an inevitable and often very emotional part. I believe that we have all died many times and will continue to live and die. Our path is defined by our accumulated intentions. Death is a fact of life in a material sense, although I believe that our energy transforms itself, or reincarnates.

At first, reincarnation was difficult for me to

accept, and I probably risk losing some readers by discussing it. It is hard enough to accept that it is possible to heal people without touching them or even meeting them. I am not a Buddhist and I haven't read much on Buddhism. My views on reincarnation come solely from my insights and ability to see the past lives of others and myself.

I believe that we have each had many lives in the past. Sometimes, our illnesses have something to do with our past lives. I also believe that some of the scars we obtain throughout our lifetime are related to something that happened to us when we were in a previous life.

Many people have experienced déjà vu, the feeling that you've experienced that same experience before. Many people when visiting another country for the first time feel a deep connection, as though they'd been there before. Or upon meeting someone for the first time you may have a sense of familiarity, as if you have known that person for a long time. Sometimes it is an uneasiness you feel when meeting someone, almost like a fear of being around them that you cannot explain. Then there are the times you find yourself coming up with information you never realized you knew. I believe that these are indications that this life is not our first.

I am actually able to see many of the past lives that people have experienced. When I go in to someone, I usually see present injuries as well as old injuries. I have yet to find someone who doesn't have something wrong with them. However, every person has a bright white light inside which I can go into. Inside this white light, I see what looks like a pure body with no scars or injuries. Maybe this represents what we refer to as the soul. From this bright light I am able to access a person's past lives. There are so many past lives that I seem to access a different one each time I go in. When I see these past lives, I receive vivid details. I looked at my dad and saw him at war with troops that carried a British flag with a battalion number. I have also seen him as a fisherman who lost his life at sea. My dad has always been terrified of swimming in deep water, and I don't think that this fear is coincidental.

Sometimes our past lives are not what we might want them to be. I went into the past life of a friend and saw that he had been a sheep farmer. There is nothing wrong with being a sheep farmer, but most people expect something more glamorous. They want to have been a king or queen in a past life. Whatever your past consists of, it makes up the person you are now. You are like a quilt fabricated from many different patterns to make something that is beautiful.

OPEN-MINDEDNESS

As with any form of healing, if you are not open to the idea of it being successful, it very likely won't be. We all have the ability to close our minds and therefore narrow the outcome possibilities of any experience. Conversely we can be open-minded enough to accept the possibility of positive change.

A person can be both open-minded and skeptical at the same time. You have to be careful that you don't become so committed to skepticism that your ability to be open-minded is lost. Good researchers have open and inquiring minds. There is no shortage of published formal scientific studies to support the validity of distant healing. Yet, the mere mention of distant healing to most people is considered almost taboo. Even people who profess to be open-minded have no interest in learning about it.

It is difficult for me to face this rejection from people, since I experience my special gift every day. It has fueled my ambition to educate and inform the world about the existence of these abilities. Many scientific inventors were ridiculed by their contemporaries. It was only later in their lives that they became great men and women in the eyes of the world.

Take Alexander Graham Bell, for instance. In 1876, he invented the telephone but had difficulty finding anyone interested in it. Chief engineer Sir William Preece at *British Post* said, "England has plenty of small boys to run messages." Sir William Preece was a Fellow of the Royal Society who had studied under the great chemist and physicist Michael Faraday. Sir Preece outdid this judgment when Thomas Edison announced that he had invented an electric light. Preece said it was "a completely idiotic idea."

But the best example of all has to be the Wright brothers. Although they had photographs of them flying their plane and held many public demonstrations which local dignitaries attended, their invention was dismissed as a hoax by most American scientists and top science magazines.

There are several memorable quotes from skeptics. Prominent British mathematician and physicist Lord Kelvin stated in 1895 that "heavier-than-air flying machines are impossible." A couple of years later he said, "Radio has no future." An editorial in the *Boston Post* in 1865 proclaimed, "Well informed people know it is impossible to transmit the voice over wires and that were it possible to do so, the thing would be of no practical value." In 1899, Charles H. Duell, U.S. Commissioner of Patents, made this statement: "Everything that can be invented has been invented." And finally, Thomas Watson, chairman of IBM, said, "I think there is a world market for maybe five computers."

Thankfully, my search has led to a number of

well-educated people who are very knowledgeable and willing to help me understand my healing ability. They are courageous people. It takes a strong individual to go against mainstream thinking and pursue answers to the many unexplained events around us. I truly respect these people and hope they will be vindicated someday from all the attacks by their critics.

It is interesting how people whom I have known all my life are so doubtful when I explain distant healing. But it is reassuring that most people can eventually understand and accept this concept. I have changed the thinking of many people simply by demonstrating what I do. When people actually feel sensations in their body from a distant healing and notice a definite change in their health, they find it difficult to deny that it works. Of course, there are people who are skeptics just for the sake of being skeptical. I almost feel an obligation to change their thinking, because it seems like such a shame for someone to go through life and miss out on something so simple yet so profound. There is joy in the healing of a person, and there is also joy from changing a person's views on distant healing. I am unable to heal everyone, but I can make people aware of the existence of this connection, which we all potentially have access to. The "Seven Steps for Life" outlined in the next chapter will help you unlock your own self-healing ability.

How do you see the relationship of healing to spirituality or the soul?

Healing is far more than a physical experience. Emotions and spirit can and should be part of the healing experience. It is arbitrary to separate emotional, physical and spiritual realms of yourself. They are all interconnected and intertwined as one experience. Creating a positive frame of mind will propel you in your healing journey.

Are emotional issues related to physical ailments?

Which came first: the chicken or the egg? Emotional issues can create energy blockages that may eventually physically manifest as a problem. Physical ailments can cause a plethora of psychological issues. It is important to address them together as being integral parts of you. Your emotional and physical being is one. Improving your health and well-being is only complete if you can reflect on your total self.

Does one have to believe in order for energy healing to work?

Energy healing works through the intentions of the healer and the person being healed. If that person doubts it will make a difference, this may affect the outcome. It is important to keep an open mind in order for any form of healing to take place.

Chapter 9

Living Well with the
Seven Steps for Life

Everything is interconnected,
so one change affects everything else.

—ADAM

*I*t is essential that we find happiness in our everyday lives. A positive approach to life and all that it brings will ensure that good things happen. And this in turn equates with better health. Research has shown that not only are levels of stress hormones reduced in people with a positive attitude, but their wounds heal significantly faster than those of people who feel negative. Positive feelings make the immune system stronger and give it direction. Negative feelings and emotions have been shown to weaken the immune system.

Difficulties and challenges are daily occurrences, and severe problems occur from time to time. What makes a difference to the outcome is not so much the details of the problem but how you perceive and handle the problem. *How* you react to something is more important than *what* is happening. And that's where people have much more power and control than they realize. You always have a choice as to how you are going to react. And your choice can often, if not always, strongly influence the outcome.

You can always choose your attitude. Your attitude determines how you react to something. It also determines how much stress is attached to a situation. People bring much more stress into their lives than they need to, simply by reacting inappropriately to situations. By choosing a positive attitude—a positive reaction—you can immediately diminish your stress levels. Few situations in life merit an over-the-top reaction. It is better to learn to relax, go with the flow, and enjoy the simple pleasures of life.

It is also helpful if you can approach life with a sense of humor. Kids are naturals at this. The average kid laughs or chuckles about 145 times a day.

The average adult does this only about four or five times a day. A big difference!

Children also know how to enjoy the simple pleasures of life, such as splashing in puddles. This is because they have a different concept of time and its passing. It wouldn't occur to young children to concern themselves that they might get wet or dirty from puddle-splashing. They live in the moment of the fun, appreciating the present, the now. Future concerns, consequences and worries don't even enter their psyche. Children live in the present. Somehow over time we lose this perspective, yet it is essential for maintaining health.

I believe it is lost when our lives become controlled by time. We start school at a certain age during a certain time of year, on a predetermined day, at a prescheduled time. Time is all of a sudden of extreme importance to us, even though our understanding of it is still vague.

In school, some days pass quickly. For me, it's sports days. On other days, time slows down, as when we are being taught something in which we are not the least bit interested. Time varies a great deal on the same day, depending on our interest level in the activity. The academic part of school usually passes slowly, but then lunchtime passes so quickly that sometimes we hardly have time to eat, let alone get a good game of ball going, before the bell rings and it's back to class.

For me and many of my classmates, the afternoon in school has to be the slowest that time could possibly move without standing still. By this time, most kids have had enough of sitting. Finally the bell rings, and happy yelps of freedom echo through the hallways. The next couple of hours skip by in seconds before we have to be home for dinner.

Gradually, we learn how to tell time, and most kids eventually get a watch, and consider it an essential item to have with them at all times. We are no longer told what time it is by the sound of the school bell ringing or the turning on of the streetlights. Time is now a precise measurement. No longer does our mother gently wake us from our dream state. We have now grown up enough to have our own alarm clock scream in our ears at a designated time. Each day starts with an incredible and unnatural adrenaline shock to our system.

As we become adults, we are conditioned to equate time with money. We are expected to get jobs that have specific hours of work. The normal workday starts at 9 A.M., lunch is noon to 1 P.M., and the day ends at 5 P.M. So the workday schedules our time and events for five days out of every week. Here's the schedule of a typical, albeit simplified, weekday:

7:00 A.M.	Alarm clock rings, wake up, shower
7:30 A.M.	Breakfast
8:00 A.M.	Catch the bus or drive to work
8:45 A.M.	Get to work early, looking sharp!
9:00 A.M.	Workday begins
12:00 P.M.	Hungry or not, it's lunchtime
1:00 P.M.	Back to work
5:00 P.M.	Workday ends, commute home begins
5:30 P.M.	Get home, start making dinner
6:00 P.M.	Eat, whether hungry or not
6:30 P.M.	Chores and evening activities

| 10:00 P.M. | Wind down so we can wake up at |
| 7:00 A.M. | And start the whole thing again |

In short, we wake at a specific time, rather than when our bodies tell us that we feel adequately rested. Many people keep functioning without enough sleep, relentlessly keeping in stride with the clock. Functioning this way is a major contributor to stress. Fatigue is epidemic in our society and leads to errors in judgment, accidents, strained relationships, frayed nerves and deteriorating health.

We eat at the designated time, not necessarily when we are hungry. If you ask some people if they are hungry, they will look at their watch before they answer. Eating becomes an activity within our off time. This may lead to overeating as a habit or social pastime. It is seen as beyond something that our bodies require. This may result in addictive behavior, which can lead to obesity, a growing health problem in our society. Eating can easily become a comfort-zone activity during scheduled timeout. Then it becomes an activity we treasure because it is beyond the bounds of our stressful time-constrained day.

Many notions of measuring time create stress for us. In school, exams must be written at specific times, which may not be the time of day at which we function most effectively. But we do it to avoid failing; we must keep up with our grades.

People who have been told by their doctors that they are terminally ill are given a death sentence. Many people who are told they have only six to twelve months to live will take that as an indisputable fact and die within this prescribed time. We tend to forget that nobody knows this as fact and of all people on earth, *you* have the most to say and do about this. Indeed, it is well known in the medical field that some patients will hang on to life until they are able to see someone important or significant to them. Earlier I mentioned a man who recovered sufficiently from a stroke until all his significant family members were able to come see him. This often happens. We have more control over our conscious and subconscious thoughts than we are often led to believe.

The point is, if we don't want to hear something, we can always choose not to listen. If something is doing us psychological harm, such as being told that we are going to die in six months, we can deflect it. Always take the opportunity to empower yourself. You have the power until or unless you choose to give it to someone else.

We can learn a great deal from little children about the importance of time. Almost all preschoolers could give us the following valuable advice, through their actions: Let time be. This is particularly hard for type-A personalities, or high-strung individuals, but the best thing they could do is leave their watches at home. Our societal obsession with creating structured time is the ultimate source of many illnesses. Time is structured only through the eye of the beholder: You!

The Seven Steps for Life that follow will help you unlock your self-healing ability. At first glance they may appear simplistic. Sometimes the most important observations are the most obvious, and often the most overlooked. Read this information carefully and objectively examine what changes you can make to your life for your maximum benefit.

SEVEN STEPS FOR LIFE
Step 1: Feel Your Own Energy and Be Aware of It

To feel your own energy, rub your palms together in a circle. Be sure to rub the spot right in the center of your palms. Feel the generation of heat. It is your energy. Then hold your palms an inch or two apart and feel the magnetic push and pull. Move your palms farther apart, until you can no longer feel your energy field. Play with your energy and have fun with it. Our energy system is what this is all about, so become aware of it.

This flow of energy is our life force. It is more important than any other single body system because it involves all of them. Yet, our digestive, respiratory, circulatory, metabolic and nervous systems are better known in Western medicine. We have created lots of tests to measure the efficiency and health level of each of these. We have yet to develop a measurable level for our energy system, and so it is ignored. Yet, it directly affects all aspects of our health. Learn to feel it, work with it and, most of all, enjoy it.

Step 2: Breathe Abdominally and Be Aware of It

Breathe deeply. Many people usually breathe shallow breaths, from their chests, and are actually somewhat oxygen deprived. Breathing using your diaphragm and abdominal muscles promotes relaxation and reduces tension. Athletes and singers require lots of oxygen intake and this is the method of breathing that they use. The body gets enough to function, but would function even better with deep, full breaths. Singers and athletes are very aware of how proper breathing enhances their performance. We all need air in order to reach our maximum potential.

Breathe in through your nose and imagine filling your abdomen with air. Once full, exhale through your mouth and pull in your belly. Your shoulders should not go up and down with breathing. It may take a bit of time for you to develop good breathing habits, but stick with it. I know some people who make a point of deep breathing on their daily walk. They count to four as they inhale, hold for another four counts and then breathe out over four counts. This is a good exercise to practice proper breathing. Increase the number of counts as your lung capacity expands over time.

Step 3: Ground Your Energy and Be Aware of Its Flow

It is important to ground your energy often. Think of your energy as circulating through and around you, connecting you to the universal energy above and below the earth. With each breath, breathe in air and energy from above and around you. When exhaling, imagine forcing that energy down the front of your body, through the soles of your feet to the center of the earth. Feel your soles connecting to the earth's core. The exhale connects you to everything on the planet. The inhale connects you with all in the universe. This is grounding, which is all about being aware of our connection to energy systems. Grounding will increase your physical energy and strength by unifying your aura with other energy systems. It will cleanse your aura and generally improve your health.

Step 4: Drink Water

Drink water. Lots of it! Our bodies are nearly 80 percent water—it composes that much of our body weight. We are water-based creatures, and we must respect this. Every day, drink the eight glasses your body needs. Drink filtered water, if possible. If you want a more exciting taste, add a twist of fresh lime or lemon.

Our bodies need water to operate optimally. If we face an additional health challenge because of an injury or illness, water is a vital part of our recovery. Our bodies remove unwanted and unnecessary materials by excreting them along with the water. This is our natural purification process. Without water, toxins that could easily be removed on a regular basis accumulate in our bodies. Dehydration can be deadly.

Consuming water is the easiest habit to change, and the most overlooked. Water is readily available to most of us and sometimes can alone achieve remarkable results. You would never think of trying to run your car without adding oil and gas. Why would you treat your car with more respect and care than you would your own body? We have been given this fabulously effective body, and it shouldn't be taken for granted.

Step 5: Develop Emotional Bonds with Others

Many of us, but not all, are fortunate enough to have loving family members. And, at any moment in time, each and every one of us has the opportunity to bond with others as friends. We all need these emotional connections. It requires a give-and-take of trust to make relationships work, but it is well worth the effort. Welcome it, and your world becomes a wonderful, loving place to live, a place filled with good, harmonious energy.

Stable and loving relationships have been shown to have a strong and positive influence on health. Those who have made the effort and commitment to develop close relationships with family members and friends are healthier than those who lack these relationships. If they do get sick or injured, they recover much faster than people who do not have a network of supportive family or friends.

Step 6: Think Positively in the Present Tense and Feel Its Effects

The power of your own positive thoughts helps balance your mental, physical, emotional and spiritual aspects. This balance empowers us, making us able to achieve our dreams and keep us healthy. Stay in the now, as the past is over and, although it is good to have dreams, fears about the future are futile.

Dream of what you truly love to do and do it. Only *you* can make a lasting change in yourself. By looking inward, it is possible to re-create yourself. Be aware of your feelings and your power to adjust and control them.

Put yourself into a quiet meditative state. Picture a three-dimensional holographic image of yourself. This takes lots of concentration and practice. Make it an exact image of yourself. If your eyes are blue, imagine the image of yourself having blue eyes. Visualize it. Concentrate on seeing your eyes exactly as they are. Work on perfecting this image until it is an exact image of you, exact in every detail. Even someone who lacks imagination can do this.

Once you have this clear image in your mind, repeat to yourself that you are all better and problem-free. Concentrate this beam of positive thoughts on the injured area. For example, if you have an elbow problem, project these positive thoughts like a laser beam toward your elbow.

Do not think of the problems. You do not have any problems in the image you have put in front of you. Think of the perfect hologram, one with no injuries. I know this can work for you because of what I do. I heal people with my ability to connect to their energy holograms. Once I connect to a person, I use my thoughts to perform the healing work that I do.

I understand that this ability to connect to a person's hologram is a gift. I also know that we all have the ability to make the connection to our own holograms and use the power of thought to heal. This does not come easily, but with the desire to learn and with some practice, you will succeed. By continuing to practice, you will find that it gets easier and easier, and that your ability to do this increases. Once you master it, you will find this an effective method of improving and maintaining your state of wellness.

Step 7: Understand and Appreciate the Connectedness of Everyone and Everything

Everything affects everything else in the entire universe in a weblike manner. Positive thoughts and actions taken by one of us affect everyone else. While the people most affected are those closest to us in the web—family, friends, workmates and acquaintances—the entire web is indeed affected. It is this interconnectedness that enables distant healing to take place.

Feel grateful for your life—it is precious. Be thankful for all the wonderful people who have connected with you along your journey. Look forward to the adventures that each day brings. We all face challenges, but our attitude as we face them makes all the difference. The positive outlook of each of us is contagious.

The Seven Steps for Life will help guide you along your personal journey to wellness. Use them as a motivational guide to keep you on course with your healing journey. Keep them handy and get in the habit of referring to them often as a useful reminder of the essential steps for your health.

Seven Steps for Life

1. Feel your energy and be aware of it. Make it a habit to feel your life force energy daily.
2. Breathe abdominally and be aware of it. Practice this every chance you get until it becomes second nature.
3. Ground your energy and be aware of its flow. This can be done any time of the day and anywhere, such as when you are standing in line at a store.

4. Drink water. Make a mental note of every time you have treated yourself to a glass of water.

5. Develop emotional bonds with others. Be consciously aware of doing something positive to make another person's day a little better.

6. Think positively in the present tense and feel its effects. Make a point of relaxing peacefully at some point throughout your day, whether in a state of meditation or self-reflection.

7. Understand and appreciate the connectedness of everything and everyone. Express appreciation for one thing that you are grateful for each and every day. Feel gratitude, smile and be happy.

Chapter 10

Your Dream

*People have much more power
and control than they realize.*

—ADAM

the response I get from people when I tell them of
my abilities. If someone asks me to explain my ability, I might say, "I do distant healing by connecting
to the quantum hologram of another person."
Some friends and relatives whom I have known
almost all my life have reacted in a similar
manner—either dismissing the subject or deflect-
ing it with a response along the lines of, "Lovely
weather we're having, isn't it?"

Those who are receptive and understand what I
do often find themselves in the same predicament
as me, trying to explain it to others. It's almost as if
it is taboo to talk about something that doesn't fit
mainstream thinking. We all have to change this
mentality in order for humankind to advance at a
conscious level—the level of knowing and understanding everything within us and around us.

Usually, people need to be alone with me before
they will engage in a conversation on the topic.
When there is more than one person present, a
giggle factor often kicks in. It is a form of human
self-defense when our brains can't stretch far
enough to grasp an idea or concept.

Accepting change or a new way of thinking is referred to as a paradigm shift. There have been many examples of dramatic paradigm shifts throughout civilization, and there is no reason to believe that there won't be many more. I always thought that one characteristic of humankind that prevents us from moving forward is ego. A dramatic example of how ego can have a major impact on how we perceive things is the Ptolemaic system, which came about in the second century A.D. Scientists, accepting the view of Greek astronomer and geographer Ptolemy, claimed that the universe rotated around the earth. With billions and billions of stars and planets in the sky, how much bigger can one's ego be? But nonetheless, this scientific proclamation was widely accepted.

The Ptolemaic system was so entrenched in medieval society that many people were put to death for thinking differently. We might find that shocking, but what it really should do is remind us that we must continue to question today's science and not just accept it. We must always be able to subjectively analyze knowledge beyond our current scientific base of information. We should learn from our past and not blindly accept all current science as truth. We've been mistaken before.

If you tether an elephant to a small post with a rope that is simply placed over the top of the post, the elephant is unable to move away. Despite that it is not tied, and even though the elephant with its massive weight could easily pull the post from the ground, the elephant will not move. In its mind, it thinks that it is securely tethered and can't possibly pull away. Obviously, that couldn't be further from the truth, because all the elephant has to do is walk away. This analogy can easily be applied to our day-to-day thinking about what is possible and impossible. Our limitations are self-imposed.

There is a swell of change taking place in the world today. With freedom comes the ability to question the medical and scientific dogma that we confront on a daily basis. It wasn't long ago that you wouldn't dare tell your doctor that you would like a second opinion. Today, many doctors go out of their way to explain their medical diagnoses in detail in order to meet the demands of inquiring patients. This is, in a small way, a paradigm shift. People are finally coming to the realization that doctors really aren't gods (though their opinions should be respected). Ultimately, health choices are one's own responsibility.

More and more of us are becoming aware of people with special abilities. There are many things that we don't understand and science cannot yet explain. We are coming to the realization that if science can't explain something, that doesn't mean it's impossible. Another belief that is tough to change is that experts are all open-minded and willing to explore science. Even top scientists have paradigms they don't want to breach. Change is difficult and humans resist change. However, we must change in order to move forward, and this will happen naturally when the critical mass of consciousness is reached. This means that when enough people become aware of our connectedness, our conscious awareness will change with it.

One force joins us. One idea keeps us apart. Love is the unifying force. Fear is the underlying separation of beings. The future of humankind depends on how we apply this unifying force. Love and cooperation is needed.

Fear and material competition must be left in the past with ego. They only intensify our perception of separateness, which leads to conflict. Human survival is the ultimate goal of every being and can be accomplished when our commonality, not our differences, is our focus.

My goal is to make people realize that many things exist that are beyond our five senses. We have to be able to open our mind's eye and see beyond the societal and scientific paradigms that exist in our world. Everyone must become fully aware of our interconnectedness. Only then will we be able to heal ourselves. Believe in yourself and everything becomes possible. There is more to this universe than we know.

Stay tuned!

DreamHealer 2

A Guide to Healing and Self-Empowerment

DreamHealer is the story of a teenager called Adam and his discovery that he could heal others. He has the ability to connect to, and influence, another person's health – whether they are on the same continent or not makes no difference whatsoever.

In *DreamHealer 2*, Adam shares the secrets of his gift, teaching the reader how to tap into their own healing abilities through the use of visualisation techniques.

DreamHealer 3

*The Quantum World
of Energy Healing*

Adam has healed many people and helped many people with the healing of themselves: his mother's MS when he was fourteen, himself when he fractured his spine and many other people who share their stories in the book. At his popular workshops held throughout North America, he teaches people how to effectively focus their own healing intentions for self-empowerment. His unique group treatments, which involve all attendees, are the highlight of these events.

In *DreamHealer 3*, Adam shares his thoughts, observations and wisdom that is often far beyond his years. He describes how the mysteries of healing are connected with science and spirituality as one.